Out Of Darkness

Out of Darkness
Copyright 2016, Jaki Parlier
10402 Oronsay Circle
Huntington Beach, CA 92646

Book Design by Tanya J Charfauros
Cover Design and illustration by Tanya J Charfauros
 ~*Linoleum carving print on Shutterstock watercolor image*
Photography by Desiree Carnell, Nan Cunningham, Leah Foster, Roger Thiele, Jim Parlier, Dennis DeMoss, Gweni Hetzel, Lyle Wyse, Steve Anderson, Joe Anderson, Joel LaBret, Ukarumpa Media

All Scripture references are from the Holy Bible.

Printed in the United States of America by Headwaters Christian Resources. www.headwatersresources.org

ISBN: 978-1-945413-91-9

Dedication

Dedicated with love to my three amazing children,

Rick, Randy and Tanya.

Born in the beautiful town of Lae in Papua New Guinea, you spent your growing up years with the Managalasi people of Numba Village.

By learning to speak the Managalasi language, eating village food and hunting in the jungle, you have endeared yourselves to these people forever.

Your skills in their cultural activities have also strengthened our relationship with the Managalasi people, binding all of us together as one loving family.

The memory of you squatting before an open fire roasting food with your friends on our front porch will live forever in my mind.

Tanya, you were the answer to the prayers of women when, just before I boarded the plane for Lae to give birth, they begged me: *Bring home a baby girl this time!* Your gentle, lovable ways brightened all our lives.

I love you, Rick, Randy and Tanya, and will remain proud of you and grateful to be your mother till the day the Lord calls me Home.

Left to right: Randy, Tanya and Rick

Foreward

Pastor Roger Thiele
Curlew Community Church, Curlew, WA USA

> *Then Jesus came to them and said, "All author-*
> *ity in heaven and on earth has been given to me.*
> *Therefore go ..." Matthew 28:18–19a (NIV)*
> *Jesus answered and said to him, "If anyone loves*
> *me, he will keep my word ..." John 14:23a (NASB)*

By the year 2004, the God of grace and mercy had long since been at work in the hearts of the people living on the Managalasi plateau in the beautiful country of Papua New Guinea. Coming to teach a three week course at the recently established Ese Bible Institute in Numba Village, I soon realized that I had been brought there to receive some profound teaching myself.

During this visit I saw firsthand how Jesus uses people to fulfill His promise to be in the midst of those gathered in His Name. It was evident that Jim and Jaki Parlier's relationship with the villagers was the witness through which the God of grace and mercy revealed His great plan of love and redemption. These two faithful servants exhibited the sacrificial care of Jesus Christ to those who hunger and thirst for His righteousness.

Establishing the Ese Bible Institute in this remote area of Oro Province was not a task for the faint of heart nor one easily discouraged. As a result of this missionary couple's single-minded vision of obedience to God by teaching His

Word and practicing His love, our Lord has transformed thousands of souls through the power of His Name. The Parliers demonstrated to me that we, as ordinary people, can do all things through Christ, who is the living God. For this I am eternally thankful to my friends Jim and Jaki and grateful to our amazing God who ordained it.

May this book be a blessing to you as it recounts the grace of God at work in the people of Papua New Guinea through the lives of Jim and Jaki Parlier and the Ese Bible Institute.

*"If you abide in Me, and My words abide
in you, ask whatever you wish, and it shall
be done for you." John 15:7 (NASB)*

They went out for the sake of the Name — and He is forever faithful!

Pastor Roger Thiele with his two right-hand men, Pastors Michael and Chululu who are the key leaders in translation, literacy and the Ese Bible Institute. In the middle is Pastor Michael's daughter Mercy.

Acknowledgments

My thanks to Gretchen Pasantino-Coburn for her helpful suggestions as I labored towards the end of writing this book. Working with her has been a short but insightful journey.

I'm indebted to my friend and mentor Martha McNeill who made smooth my writing in most enlightening ways. After she and her family moved to Florida, we continued working together via the postal system, but I missed her smile and unfailing source of strength that came with previous face-to-face contact.

After I began volunteering for The Seed Company, I made contact with writer/editor Jenny Evans who has accompanied me through most of the chapters. I appreciated her thoroughness in editing and the wise suggestions she offered.

Nearing completion of the book I met Roxanne Tretheway, she had done editing work for Ariel Ministries, a Jewish-Christian ministry, and others. Her excellent comments have taught me new and efficient techniques.

Unending thanks to Tanya Jill Charfauros, daughter extraordinaire, who illustrated the cover and designed the chapter breaks throughout the book. Her encouragement gave me the push needed to finish writing this miracle story of what God has accomplished on the Managalasi Plateau.

Heartfelt thanks to Carson Cunningham, son of Nan and Gene, for providing colorful shirts to each Ese Bible Institute (EBI) graduate. As of 2016, the graduates number 365.

We are blessed to have Joe Anderson, one of the EBI teachers, be a part of God's miracle to Numba Village, and also for his help with the printing of this book. It's our hope that those who read it will be encouraged to trust God more and be challenged to serve Him.

Lastly, thanks always to my husband Jim who read each chapter and then gave me the high sign indicating his approval. His being a part of this journey added significant meaning to this accomplishment, and I am grateful for his encouragement.

OUT OF DARKNESS

By Jaki Parlier

Table of Contents

Chapter 1

A Cross Too Heavy

Wednesday, May 31, 1995, the day I'd been dreading for more than a year, had begun. Whenever my thoughts turned to this day, a band of pressure tightened around my chest and squeezed. Today was the day Jim and I would return to Papua New Guinea (PNG) after living in America for 14 years.

Prior to that, Jim and I had spent 20 years living among the Managalasi people; we had learned their language, created an alphabet, taught them to read and write, and then finally translated the New Testament into their language.

For the past year I repeatedly asked myself, *Why will it be so difficult to return to the land I love? To the people I love and desperately long to see again?*

During the years of learning the language and culture, translating and teaching, the Managalasi people had become family. Returning to them after 14 years should feel like going home.

But it didn't. Why?

Although I knew the answer, I continually asked myself the same question, as if by some miracle the old days would return—the days when our children Rick, Randy and Tanya lived with us. Returning without them today was too painful to think about.

All three were born in PNG and had contributed to the

strong relationship we had with these people in many ways. The Managalasi village was *their* home too, and the Managalasi people were their family. Rick and Randy spoke the language as well as Jim and I. They even knew the names of birds and trees that we had never bothered to learn.

Another concern was, *What would the Managalasis think when we got off the plane and they didn't see their beloved Rick, Randy and Tanya? Would they be happy to see just Jim and me?*

Thoughts of the inevitable tore at my heartstrings day after day. But the kids had finished college now and were settled into their own lives. Rick, our older son, was a Marine stationed in San Diego. Randy worked with the Jet Propulsion Lab as a computer engineer. Our youngest, Tanya, had just married and was working as a graphic artist with The Seed Company, an affiliate of Wycliffe Bible Translators.

For years the Managalasi people had been writing letters begging us to come back and revise their New Testament. "We don't talk this way anymore," they lamented. "Our language has changed. It's the young people—they don't understand a lot of the old words. Please come back, live with us again, and put the talk into the language we speak today."

The younger generation objected strongly to the vocabulary the older people used when we translated years ago. Many words were foreign to them—the ancient words having been pushed from their culture by the entrance of the western world with its new customs and terms.

Ted, Tanya's husband, had borrowed his brother's van to drive us to the airport in Los Angeles. Rick, Ted and Tanya,

and Randy, with his friend Lorina, took the day off from
their places of work to come to the airport to bid us farewell.
During the drive on the 405 Freeway, my thoughts turned
to life in the village in those long-ago days—how the kids
adopted the culture so easily, how they learned to speak the
Managalasi language so well, how they learned to love their
brown-skinned friends so much.

Time will pass quickly, I told myself, trying to patch the
hole in my heart. *At least we won't have to learn the language,*
I reasoned. *The revision should be done in no time. Maybe
we'll be back before the four-year term is up....*

"Hey, Mom!" Rick called from the rear seat of the van,
returning me to the present. Only one word from Rick was
needed to detect mischief brewing. "When you get back to
the village, eat one of those bats for me!"

Hunting bats had been one of Rick's favorite things to
do. The men taught him how to use a slingshot, and Rick
became adept at the sport. He and his friends went into the
jungle almost daily and brought home fruit bats to roast
over the fire pit on our front porch.

Memories stirred, and I fought to keep the tears in check.
"I'll eat a bat only if *you're* there to eat it with me," I replied,
trying to match his playful mood.

Ted pulled up outside the Qantas terminal where we
could check our bags at the curb. I felt knots forming in
my stomach. Rick, Randy and Ted offloaded our luggage
as I stood to one side watching them pile the bags next to
the weigh-in scale. As Jim and I groped for our passports,
I heard a familiar voice calling in the distance. Martha Norris,
my special friend and colleague from Wycliffe's home office,
arrived with her fiancé, Dave McNeill. The smiles on their
faces were like a soothing ointment.

"Couldn't let you go without giving you a hug," Martha

explained warmly, putting her arm around my shoulders. *God sent them,* I realized, as we moved towards the lounge where we could all sit and chat together. The good-humored conversation diverted my mind from the impending departure, and I felt thankful to God for "His present help in my day of trouble."

We talked animatedly; I savored every moment until a voice boomed through the sound system and halted our words. It was time to board our plane. Martha and Dave stood up immediately, gave us quick hugs and left us to say goodbye to our family in private.

Suddenly, my mouth became as dry as salt. I couldn't speak past the lump growing in my throat. How would I be able to say goodbye to my children, knowing it would be four years before I would see their faces again?

There was no escaping the pain now, no more putting it off or pushing it down deep inside. *"Lord God, this cross is too heavy, I can't pick it up. Please help me through these last moments."*

After fierce hugs and encouraging words from our children, I took a deep breath and turned away quickly. With Jim close behind, I walked blindly down the ramp that led onto the plane. The image of our beloved kids bunched up together waving was vivid in my mind, raw in my heart. Knowing it was God's will to go did not ease the pain.

Jim found our seats quickly and placed our hand luggage into the upper compartment while I stood numbly by. "Take the window seat," he urged, gesturing for me to sit down. When I didn't move, he took hold of my arm and ushered me toward the window.

Soon the aircraft was being pulled backward from the tarmac. The engines revved up and we moved forward and waited for another jet to take off. A short while later we zoomed down the runway, lifting up over the Pacific Ocean, every minute taking us miles away. I fingered the note Tanya had pushed into my pocket. It was she who had the hardest time adjusting to life in America when we left Papua New Guinea and settled in California. After 14 years, I still worried about her.

In my other hand I clutched the gift Randy's friend Lorina had handed me after we hugged goodbye. I rotated the small package with my fingers and then quickly tore off the paper. There, in an antique silver frame, were their two happy faces smiling at me. Jeweled stones set into the frame winked beneath the soft cabin lights. "A perfect gift," I said aloud.

Jim turned to me with a puzzled look. I passed him the photo. As he gazed at the happy expressions on Randy and Lorina's faces, a smile cracked his fatigue-lined face.

"Orange juice?" the flight attendant asked, her eyebrows raised in question. I nodded and she handed me a glass with the liquid swishing back and forth. As I sipped the refreshing juice, I tried to push the agonizing scene at the airport from my mind. My hand slipped back into my pocket, and I pulled out Tanya's note. Unfolding it, I noted it was dated May 25th, almost a week ago:

> *Mom and Dad,*
>
> *A lot goes through my mind every day that I just keep inside. I suspect I won't be good at words the day we part, so I decided to write.*
>
> *It's hard to believe this is happening. I always encouraged you to go back to New Guinea. But maybe that's because it's what I really wanted to do — go back to Numba village. I never thought about what*

it would mean for me. Yet I know deep down in my heart that your going back is all for the best in our lives. Go back to spur the Managalasi on to more love and good deeds. They need you, and God is answering their cries through you. There might be some special lives you touch personally.

For me, I suspect Ted and I will become more "married." I'll learn to depend on him more, and more on God.

I'll miss you, Mom and Dad. Please write to me a lot!

I love you both, probably too much.

Tan

The words in her note began to still the worry on my mind. "Learn to depend on Ted more, and more on God," I mused. Then, *"in her husband's care—in God's care."*

That's how it should be. It's how God intended.

The gnawing feeling in my heart began to subside. In that moment, God gave me the assurance that my daughter would be okay.

But would I?

"And let us not lose heart and grow weary and faint in acting nobly and doing right, for in due time and at the appointed season we shall reap, if we do not loosen and relax our courage and faint." Galatians 6:9 (NASB)

"Roe nu mamaiji vehunijaho paucha'asa'avara. Ijihuni maijaho vea nimaa ro ape'eje a pasena'eje ve'amajaho ijihuni eha apehuna." Karesia 6:9

Chapter 2

Going Back Into the Future

The flight from Los Angeles to Brisbane, Australia seemed to take forever. After flying over ten hours we were more than ready to deplane. We changed planes in Brisbane and boarded a smaller jet heading for Port Moresby, the capital city of Papua New Guinea. *Port Moresby* … the very words brought a smile to my lips. We were getting close to home.

After we landed in the capital city, our translation helpers of years ago, Aparihi, also known as Pastor Michael, and Chululu, came out of nowhere, surprising us. After a joyous reunion, we took a cab to the Coffee Shop for a cold drink and to get caught up on village news. One downer was that we had to haul our luggage with us into the cab, to the Mall, up the escalator and finally into the small Coffee Shop. We were thankful for Aparihi and Chululu's help.

"Did you know we're flying to Ukarumpa on Friday?" I asked the men, still bubbling over at the sight of them.

"Yes, we knew," Chululu replied quickly. "And we hoped we could go with you!"

Hearing those words, Jim stood immediately and made his way to the phone booth down the hall. There he called the flight coordinator and booked their flights. When Friday arrived, the four of us flew to Ukarumpa, Wycliffe's center of operations. While living at the center, the four of us translated stories together and were able to finish a children's book. But the village was never far from our thoughts, and I couldn't wait to see the faces of our village friends again.

After two months passed, both men had reached the point where they felt ready to go home to their families. Jim and I, after being away from the village 14 years, felt ready, too. A few days later, the aviation bus picked us up at the curved driveway of the Guest House. Chululu and Aparihi stood grinning from ear to ear. Our anticipation matched theirs. The driver hopped down and wasted no time whisking our cargo onto the back of the bus. He was on a tight schedule. We drove away from the Guest House feeling thankful for the help the Home provided while we finalized our Children's Books at the Print Shop, packed for the village and cleaned the house for the next tenants.

Once we reached the hangar, the aviation staff quickly loaded the Cessna with our luggage. After weighing in, the four of us boarded the plane, strapped ourselves in and were ready for take-off. After flying above luscious green mountains and winding rivers for an hour and a half, I could see that familiar patch of ground cut out from thick jungle—Sila Airstrip. The strip had been cleared off to enable small planes to land in order to serve the Managalasi people during coffee selling time, and to fly in our mail and supplies as well.

Just before we landed, our Pilot Wil Benning flew low over the top of the village greeting our friends below. My heart lurched as we flew above the oval-shaped village, our home for 20 years. Having circled the village in this fashion dozens of times in the past, a feeling of flying back into the future passed over me. Small figures below waved madly, just like always.

Home … the village where we lived for more than 20 years.

They weren't merely brown-skinned figures, these people were my family. Although living half-a-world-away for 14 years, I still saw them every day—in my mind and with my heart.

Sila Airstrip, a patch of ground that's been cut out of the jungle for small planes to land.

Now we were almost home. Happiness encompassed me as I realized anew that God had given me the best of both worlds.

Ten seconds after circling, we touched down on the grassy airstrip that had just been "mowed" with machetes, and taxied up the slope to the top of the airstrip. Peering out the window I watched crowds of our Managalasi friends rushing along the sides of the airstrip to where they knew the Cessna would stop. After the engine shut down, I heard the cheers, the clapping and voices yelling "Ese!" (essay). Hearing the familiar greeting after more than a decade told me once again I had indeed stepped back in time.

Friends waiting at the side of the airstrip to welcome us home.

Excitement pulsed through me when I saw Isoro—the star reader in my first literacy class of 25 years ago. This man had a gift to learn quickly, but he had no patience for slow readers. Whenever his older brother Hwi'ura made a mistake in class, Isoro would scoff aloud at his brother: "You stupid dummy!" he'd blurt out. "Are you blind?"

Hwi'ura was unlike his brother and never retaliated.

Instead, he sat quietly with a slight smile, enduring the shame until I came to his aid.

When Isoro wasn't in the classroom, he was outside in the village acting like a policeman, constantly ordering people around, telling them what to do or where to go. Now he stood at the top of the runway, wearing a new green shirt, yelling at everyone, flailing his arms wildly, signaling people to stay in back of the airstrip boundaries. The scowl he wore made me laugh out loud. *He hasn't changed one iota,* I thought.

I stared hard through the window pane at my old student, willing him to look my way. Finally, our eyes met through the glass window, and a smile lit his face. That's when I noticed something different about him ... his teeth were white instead of the usual purplish-red color. That could only mean one thing—he wasn't chewing the psycho-stimulant *betel nut* anymore. *But he always chewed betel nut,* I thought. *What happened?*

Our patient and good-natured pilot Wil opened the door of the aircraft and we climbed down. Over 1,000 people erupted in cheers. Seconds later, we were swallowed up in hugs, perspiration, and wailing.

As Isoro clung to Jim, his expression changed once more. This time his face was scrunched up as water spilled from his eyes down both cheeks, soaking into his new shirt.

Kirija, our house worker of years ago, clung to me wailing louder than anyone. I stood clutched in his grasp for what seemed like too long and began to feel uncomfortable. My mind whirled, searching for a possible way to disentangle myself, but there was no polite way to do so. Young people stood nearby watching, their faces filled with compassion and understanding. Their reaction helped me relax.

Kirija wailed inconsolably because we were gone from his life for so many years. When we left in 1981 we managed to get him a job at the Ukarumpa Guest House. While there, he married a non-Managalasi girl from a nearby village. I remembered his letter announcing, "We named our baby boy '*Parlier*,' after Jim."

Suddenly, I realized God was using the sad expressions of the young people surrounding us to remind me that embracing and crying loudly in this culture was the way to express deep emotion—that I was back in *their* culture—that I had to let go of mine. Promptly, I returned Kirija's hug and cried with him.

Some of the women from my former Bible study stood nearby waiting patiently to greet me. Clearly they were overjoyed to see me, and I sensed the ache in their hearts because we had been apart for so long. My heart was aching, too.

Suddenly, Pastor Ivan's voice boomed: "The people in Kweno Village have prepared a special lunch for Jim and Jaki." Then, looking straight at Jim and me, he said, "The food is all ready, and they want you to come *now!*"

Kweno Village sat at the top of a round-shaped mountain with houses built around the perimeter. Whenever I visited, I was reminded of a round cake with candles on top. Jim taught weekly Bible studies in this village for years, but only a few attended. When we returned to America, there were only one or two believers there. I wondered why they would bother to prepare a special lunch now, when in years gone by they weren't interested in us, nor in learning to read, or in hearing the Gospel.

"Jaki!" Jim called out. "It's getting late, you'd better get a move on!"

Turning around, my eyes followed the trail upward to the top of the mountain. It looked like a ski slope. I was not in good physical condition and knew I would have to push mercilessly to make the trek up the steep mountain.

"Take her arm and help her!" Chululu yelled to Pupudi, his wife. Their sister-in-law Chujui was standing next to me and took my purse to carry. She flicked open her umbrella and held it over my head to provide shade. And thus I began the hike to Kweno Village with two dear friends by my side.

About a third of the way up, my legs felt wobbly and weak. I began panting heavily. "I think I'm going to have a heart attack," I said, tongue in cheek, yet wondering if perhaps I really would. The remark was not taken lightly.

Pupudi grabbed hold of my arm and held on tight. I stared into her concerned eyes. "God chose you to come back to us," she pointed out strongly. "He won't let you die now!" Her words renewed my strength, and I trudged on.

The trail stretched endlessly, each step taking more effort than I had to give. My breath felt like fire in my lungs. Chujui handed me bits of sugarcane to suck. "May God bless you and give you strength," she encouraged, the sweet smile never leaving her face.

Years ago both Pupudi and Chujui attended my Bible study faithfully. Now they were mature Christian women ministering to me. The reversed roles brought a measure of happiness to my soul.

When we reached the top of the mountain, several women smiling broadly waited with leis of freshly picked flowers. They eagerly placed the leis around our necks, Hawaiian style, greeting us with "Ese, ese!"

A large group of children stood to the side and began to sing a hymn in their language. It was a hymn we had taught the Numba Village children in Sunday School years ago. But this village had never received the hymns. *Who taught them?* I wondered as a sense of surprise and joy built up in my heart.

After the hymn, the women took us down a slight incline that led into Kweno Village. Just before entering the round-shaped village, we passed by a long building with a metal roof. Taken aback, I asked the woman beside me: "What's that building used for?"

"That's our *church!*" she said proudly. Then she explained: "After you and Jim left Papua New Guinea, the men from Numba continued to come every week and teach us about God. Now we're all believers." This news and the happiness on the woman's face sent my fatigue to the back burner.

As we moved into the village, men and women climbed down from the steps of their homes carrying steaming plates of food. "Ese Jim! Ese Jaki! Come, follow us!" they called out excitedly, gesturing towards the shelter where we would eat together. Hand-woven mats covered the bare ground. "Jim, you sit there, and Jaki here," one man said with a welcoming smile. Chatter filled the air as we sat down and were served lunch on large plates. Eating the familiar pumpkin-top greens and white yams brought on another wave of feeling that I was living in the past.

I relished the moments of togetherness, and the talk was about God: "Bible teachers from Numba Village came every Friday night just like you used to do, Jim," a church elder informed us. "More and more of us attended their meetings. After listening to their talk and understanding about Jesus, we all became believers." Jim's eye caught mine. I could tell the announcement stunned him just as it did me.

"When the Bible teachers saw that we believed," the elder continued, "they went down to the next village and taught them about God. When those people believed, they went to the next village and the same thing happened there."

Amazed, Jim and I sat humbly listening as he explained how the Word had spread from village to village. "Finally," the elder informed us, "all the villages in the area heard God's words and became believers. Each village built their own church. Today there are 45 churches in the Managalasi plateau."

What? Did I hear right? From this village of unbelievers grew 45 churches? This news was the best home-coming gift we could have received. From their excited expressions we could tell that God had indeed worked a miraculous change in their hearts and lives.

"So is My Word that goes out from My mouth: It will not return to me empty, but will accomplish what I desire and achieve the purpose for which I sent it." Isaiah 55:11 (NIV)

"Enajihuna'e Nuni ira ka'ene Nuni ira titi rene e'una va'ujaho hu vuata pauname Nuni rouna kaivo hu iraka ka'ene ve'iro va'ujaho hu veju'e marasahura." Aisea 55:11

Chapter 3

Our Welcome Home

The hike from Kweno Village to Numba involved going down a steep mountain to a shallow stream, crossing over, then climbing another steep mountain. Years back, I used the roots of small trees and other plant growth to grab hold of and pull myself up. But that was long ago—when I was younger—in better physical condition. *Would I be able to do it today? Only God knows,* I thought, and headed for the trail that led down to the water. A group of children followed close behind carrying our suitcases and the cardboard boxes filled with our supplies. Pupudi and Chujui had already gone on to Numba while we ate lunch at Kweno.

Due to the surrounding dense jungle, the pathway down to the stream was always muddy. There was never enough sun to filter through the trees and dry up the mud. Jim walked with Isoro and his friends, talking and laughing constantly. More or less left on my own, with nothing to grab onto, and no one to hold onto, I slipped and slid most of the way down the hill. When I finally reached the water, I gave a sigh of relief, concluding that it was more difficult to hike downhill than up.

After my ordeal, I decided to take a break and sit in the gushing water as though it were a giant bathtub. How refreshing it felt. The kids sat around on large rocks, chatting, giggling, and waiting patiently for me to proceed up the next mountain. I thought about the perpendicular trail that lay ahead and lingered in the water as long as I dared. Then I heard Jim's voice breaking into my reverie.

"Jaki! Get a move on! The Numba people are waiting!"

"Mamako!" (Hurry up!) Isoro agreed, back to being his old bossy self.

Replying would have used too much energy, so I wordlessly got up out of the water, and, dripping wet, did my best to "get a move on." My clothes stuck to my body, but, too weary to care, I braced myself to press onward.

As we started up the mountain, I heard the children murmuring under their breath: "Numba people are coming, Numba people are coming." Then I heard voices on the trail ahead. Sure enough, four young men came trotting down the mountain towards us. Together they carried some sort of contraption. *What's that?*

"Jaki, we've come to get you," one of the men said as the group approached me. He set down part of the cumbersome device to grasp my hand. "Ese," he greeted. "We made a chair to carry you to Numba."

"What?" I exclaimed, aghast that these men planned to carry me up a mountain in a makeshift chair. Upon closer scrutiny, I saw that they had built a platform of round bamboo poles tied together with vine. Fastened to the platform was a plank of wood with legs and a backrest.

"We don't want you to have a heart attack walking up these mountains," the man said. I marveled anew at how fast news traveled without the use of telephones. Then the light dawned: *Pupudi and Chujui hadn't deserted me after all. They went ahead to get someone to come back and help me over these mountains.* God bless them!

I looked closely at one of the men. His face looked so

familiar. "Are you Kwaare?" I stammered.

His smile came quickly. "Yes," he admitted. "When I heard that my mother was out of breath walking up the mountain, I got some of the other men to help make this carrier. Come, sit down on it. I'll help you."

Kwaare was Rick and Randy's friend all through their growing-up years. Along with my sons, he, too, called me *Mom*. Now Kwaare was as tall as Jim, strong and lean, and sported a mustache. As I grasped his hand, another brief moment of living in the past overtook me.

Feeling unsure of myself, I stepped onto the bamboo platform and sat down before I let go of Kwaare's hand. *Was I really as decrepit as I felt?* Promptly, the four men squatted, grabbed hold of one corner of the platform, then each, ejecting a sound like they were lifting a ton, raised me up. Without wasting a moment, they started uphill. We moved quickly, and I felt as if I were riding on an old dilapidated bus.

We rounded some hairpin turns, and my body went rigid as I clung to the sides of the bench. I could hear the men's breathing coming hard and fast.

"Stop and rest!" I urged, but there was no stopping them, not until we got to the top of the mountain where the trail leveled off. Just one more mountain, and we'd be home.

Home … the village where we lived for 20 years, the place where our children grew up, where we learned to speak their language, where our friends, who used to worship ancestor spirits, now, as born again believers, lived with the assurance of eternal life.

It wasn't long before I could see the place where the trail leveled off and wound around abruptly towards the top of Numba Village. Young people holding kundu drums and rattle-like shakers waited on the curved trail. As soon as they spotted us coming, the men began beating their drums and the women shaking their shakers. When we reached the welcoming performers, my "vehicle" was lowered, and I stepped off, thanking each man profusely.

The young people love to dress up with feathers, headbands and beads for dancing.

The young people danced as they sang a traditional song just for us. First, they danced towards Jim and me, then backed away, then up towards us again, then back, at the same time ushering us into the village.

Entering Numba Village sent an intense adrenaline rush through my entire body. Even my fingers seemed to quiver. As we reached the first house, hundreds of red, purple, yellow, and pink flowers poured down on us like a storm of colorful raindrops. Older men and women waited in two long lines to greet us. It was always the old people who tugged at my heartstrings. Seeing them now brought tears to my eyes and a lump to my throat.

A group of children sang hymns in the background as we made our way through the middle of the lines, grasping the hands of these beloved friends. "We prayed for you to come back," many said with big grins, some toothless, "and now you're back!"

"Yes, we've come back," I choked out, trying to keep my emotions under control.

Saying the obvious was typical Managalasi culture, especially when greeting someone. As we embraced and cried together, I knew in my heart that we may have left our home and family in California, yet we had come home to the second family God had given us.

"I will not leave you comfortless...."

Later we enjoyed an evening meal together under the stars. No one chewed betel nut. "It wasn't good for us to chew," Isoro explained, "so we decided to give it up." Knowing how much these people loved to chew the nut, I was astounded.

Other young men who played with our children years ago told how they now held positions of leadership in the church. Some were elders, some deacons, youth workers or Sunday School teachers. Silently, I thanked the Lord for the work He had accomplished in the lives of these young men during our absence.

After we finished eating, we gathered in the church building for a specially-planned service. Men and women walked in with their worn-out New Testaments. They certainly needed new Bibles, I noted, happy to see they were reading God's Word often enough to wear the Bibles out.

Back in 1962, when no one wanted Americans to live in their village,
Benson offered us a piece of his land to build our house on.

Jim and I noticed stacks of poles and wood piled high outside the church building as we walked in. "That's the materials we gathered for your house," they told us happily. "As soon as we heard you were coming back, all the men got together and went into the jungle to cut the wood."

As the service progressed, I stood and told how much their hard work in gathering our house materials meant. "How can we ever repay you?" I asked simply.

Suddenly, it seemed like a clap of thunder struck the church and shook it with uproarious laughter. I felt confused. *What is so funny?* I wondered.

Pastor Ivan, noting my confusion, came and stood next to me on the platform. "There will be no payback," he said gently. "You are our spiritual parents, but we didn't understand that when you first came. Back then, our parents didn't want foreigners to live with us; they thought you came to steal our land. But now we know God sent you to tell us about Him and give us His Word in our language. We did wrong to make you pay for wood and food and have asked God to forgive us." His words and the gentleness with which he spoke, melted something inside me.

After the service we learned we would live in our village adopted son Joshua's house while our new home was being built. "My brother Kirija has a big house," Joshua explained to us. "So we'll just move in with him for now."

Later that night, feeling totally done in, we made our bed by flashlight. Thankfully, I dropped down onto the thin mattress, groped for my sweatshirt and wadded it up to use for a pillow. Then, from out of the blue, Jim said: "Don't think you're going to get any rewards when you get to heaven!"

My eyes flew open. I looked up at his darkened form. "What do you mean?" I asked incredulously.

"All the rewards you were going to get in heaven, you got today," he said simply.

"What are you talking about?"

"The things you heard and saw in Kweno and then in Numba are your rewards."

"You're right," I agreed.

"What's happened in this village is no different from what's happened in the villages of other translators, only we've been privileged to come back and see the fruit of our labors."

"Uh huh."

"And there went your rewards," he said, as though he was going to get his, but I wouldn't get mine.

His haughty attitude got to me. Feeling around for my flashlight, I grabbed it and shone the light on his face. That's when I saw the mischievous glint in his not-so-innocent blue eyes laughing at me.

Lying back comfortably on the thin mattress, I listened to

the fruit bats flapping their wings as they hung up-side-down in the banana trees outside; a pig grunted from underneath the house next to ours; crickets screeched; Wanauhwi River tumbled noisily over the rocks below. Listening to these familiar sounds sent me back in time once again.

Had we really left?

"Who are My mother and My brothers?" Looking about on those who were sitting around Him He said, "Here are My mother and My brothers! Whoever does God's will is My brother and sister and mother." Mark 3:33–35 (NASB)

"Nuni ohija 'ee'u'uhija irahije?" 'iamana. "Ea ka'ene Huni rori hija kaji kimapenoji'i ija 'iama "Ike kiha! Nuni oha 'u'uhija ikena." Maka 3:33–35

Chapter 4

A Painful Submission to God's Will

I awoke to the sound of the conch shell vibrating across the church yard and up into the village. Years ago, this same sound echoed from mountain to mountain to warn of enemy attacks. Today, blowing the conch shell alerts people that church services or village meetings are about to begin.

Blowing the conch shell announces that it's time for meetings to begin.

A slight feeling of alarm crept up inside me. "What day is it?" I asked Jim.

"It's Tuesday morning, time for your women's prayer meeting and Bible study," he replied with eyebrows raised, as if to ask what I was going to do. He knew I didn't have time to prepare a message for the women yet.

My heart sank. I had forgotten about the early Tuesday morning prayer meetings. "What'll I teach?" I moaned.

"Oh, just tell them how happy you are to be back," he suggested as he combed his hair. "They'll understand that you didn't have time to prepare." He put his comb in his pocket and turned towards the door. "I'll go find Chris and have him carry in a bucket of warm water so you can take your shower and get going."

"Check and see if there's enough firewood to heat the water," I yelled after him, but it was unnecessary. Chris, who had begun working for us as a teenager and was now married and a father of two, had already heated the water and earlier had carried it up from the river. Jim directed him to pour some of the hot water into a bucket for me.

As I washed, I wondered what I would share. Surely the women would be expecting me to teach something from God's Word. I reflected on how some of the women used to skip prayer meetings; other things, like garden work, got in the way. Maybe I should encourage them to be faithful to pray every Tuesday morning, and then think about doing their garden work later. Yes! That's it! *Putting God first* would be a good lesson to begin with.

At 8:30 the sun was already hot and warmed my back as I walked across the grass from Joshua's house to the church building. Evidence of God's creation surrounded me—mountains, vibrant flowers with multi-colored butterflies flitting around, and the many palm trees. Unlike my Managalasi friends, I grew up in the concrete jungle of Newark, New Jersey, and therefore would never take such beauty for granted.

My mind flew back to the task at hand. *I could also remind the women how Paul met Lydia and then the Philippi church got started—all because women got together and prayed.* Prayer is no small thing; it is important, and God uses women who pray to accomplish His work.

Yes, I'll challenge them with that, I concluded, feeling more confident about what I would be sharing with them in just a short while.

When I entered the church, the women had just finished singing a hymn. Chujui stood in front with a serious expression. "Pitopito," she said, "you pray for the high school students who are at school in Popondetta." Popondetta was the closest town, about a six-hour drive or a three-day walk over the mountains.

Pitopito, always ready with a warm smile, was one of my favorite friends. Her mother named her "Button" but in Managalasi it sounded like *pea lo pea lay*. Most people called her Virginia, the name given her when she was baptized in the Anglican Church.

My friend stood up immediately and began to pray. She prayed for the well-being of each student—that if they got sick, God would heal them; that if they were homesick, God would help them concentrate on their studies. Then she prayed for the parents who were left behind and missing their children, that God would help carry their sorrow; that they wouldn't think about how sad they were, but think about helping others instead.

Pitopito seemed to go on and on, praying for everything under the sun that related to the students. No stone was left unturned. In closing, she left a vivid picture in everyone's mind of the students returning for the holidays—having parties together with plenty to eat and the laughter that would fill the village. As I envisioned the reunion, I, too, was filled with happiness.

I wish I could pray like that in their language, I thought wistfully.

Others stood to pray for the country, their church, the pastors, elders and deacons. All of them prayed with the same urgency and velocity of words as Pitopito. These women knew God intimately and talked to Him believing He would answer. I felt blessed to be among them.

When prayer time finished, Chujui sat down. Bracing myself, I looked over the group wondering who would introduce me to come and speak. Instead, Kwaare's wife, a young mother of three, stood up, walked down to the front and turned to face us. She opened her Bible and read the verse about the narrow road to eternal life, and the broad way to destruction. Then she proceeded to teach the meaning of the verse with the same thoroughness and assurance with which the women prayed.

My eyes shifted around the room searching for someone who would stop and remind the woman that I was back now and would resume teaching. But no one said a word. Rather, they all sat back listening attentively.

I was dumbfounded—*Kwaare's wife was doing my teaching job!* And she was doing it very well. What Bible school had she attended? None. Instead she had married at a young age and never left the village. So, where did all this knowledge come from? The church must be teaching the people well, I concluded. Where else could she have learned to teach like this?

I could see the handwriting on the wall: the interaction I had with the women in teaching them the Word, a joy that thrilled me more than life itself, seemed to be coming to an end. The realization was difficult to accept.

I stared at Kwaare's wife, a little dazed, shaking my head as if to clear my brain from the dark thoughts that were dancing around inside it. Seeing her teach her own people was an answer to the prayers of many friends in America. Surely this is what missions is all about — training people to do the job so that after missionaries leave, the work would continue. I should have been filled with thanksgiving to God. But I wasn't.

Why not?

After the meeting ended, I greeted each lady, forcing a cheerfulness I was far from feeling.

The love we shared stemmed from God, and the roots went down deep.

Later, as I wandered home, rebellious thoughts against the very Word of God bombarded me. *Giving thanks in all things?* In all honesty, there was no way I could say *thank You* for being replaced!

"Lord," I began in protest, "You know that there's nothing that brought me more joy than teaching these women. How could I say 'thank You' for losing the privilege without being the biggest hypocrite in the world? You, Lord, would be the first to see I would be lying. "To be truthful, Lord, I don't like it. In fact, it's down-right painful. Why do You ask us to do impossible things, like 'be thankful for *all* things?'"

On and on the accusing voice assaulted my mind. My stomach felt tied in knots. I believed my wonderful relationship with these dear women was over; they didn't need me any longer.

I had almost reached the front steps of the house when another thought surfaced. "*I can do all things through Christ who strengthens me.*" This familiar verse in Philippians, the one I'd clung to and claimed all through my Bible School training years, now came to mind.

God was speaking to me!

"Okay, Lord," I breathed, "I'm going to trust You totally with this disappointment. Help me bring my will into submission to Your will. Help me keep my eyes focused on You."

Suddenly I felt my energy returning. Bounding up the steps and into the house, I was ready to face anything that came my way.

Early the next morning, as I was getting out of bed, I heard some women calling: "Jaki! Jaki! We went and got firewood for you!"

"I'm coming!" I yelled back, and dressed as quickly as I could. Hurrying outside, I found a crowd of women on the porch, their arms loaded with produce, their faces shining with big smiles of happiness.

"Jaki, ese from the Women's Club," they chorused.

Not knowing what to say, I just stood in the doorway with my mouth open.

A string bag, used for carrying food and firewood from the garden to the village, is a woman's most valuable property.

Each lady promptly took her turn presenting me with food items—yams, pumpkins, papayas, sweet potatoes. "God bless you," each said, shaking my hand. Soon I had a huge stack of produce piled at my feet, a sight worthy for a Thanksgiving Day greeting card.

As each lady laid her offering down and shook my hand, Mary, Pastor Jethro's wife, started the group singing hymns. A few prayed spontaneously, thanking Jesus for bringing me, "their mother," back to live with them again. Blinking back tears, I found a spot on the long, bamboo bench and sat down. I never experienced such a demonstration of love done just for me.

Kwaare's wife moved to sit down next to me, the love of Jesus emanating from her eyes. "If there's anything you need help with," she began, looking intently at me, "or if you have any work you can't do, just tell us and we'll help you." The tenderness in her voice sent shivers of emotion creeping up my arms. Water formed on my eyelids.

"Or," she continued, "if you have a burden, let us know so we can pray, then your burden will become our burden, you won't have to bear it yourself, *we'll* help you."

By the time Kwaare's wife finished, I couldn't trust myself to speak. The women picked up their string bags, ready to leave. "Jaki, ese," they said.

I took a step to the edge of the porch. "Thank you," I croaked, swallowing at a huge mass in my throat. Morning sunlight streamed through the trees onto their retreating figures. They looked like angels. Some turned around and waved. "Ese!" they said again and again.

"Don't forget!" Chujui called out, "There's wood stacked up under the porch!"

These sisters in the Lord didn't just *know* the Word, they were *doers of the Word!* The feeling of oneness I'd experienced with them years ago fell over me again. I couldn't have loved them any more than at that moment.

Now I knew without a doubt I could never lose the one-ness we shared in the past, for that love stemmed from God, and the roots went down deep.

"I can do everything through Him who gives me strength."
Philippians 4:13 (NIV)

"Ene uneunecha maho'o Huni vaji Hura harura mi'eje na areri ve'eju." Piripai 4:13

Chapter 5

Our New Home

After living in Joshua's house for three months, our new home was ready to move into. Kingston, his pretty wife Matilda and their three children would be our neighbors. Our houses were built across the grassy field from the church, a few feet below the village. The narrow pathway that wound down the mountain to Wanaohwi River was the dividing line between our properties.

While building the house, Jim worked with Kingston and several other men. One day Kingston surprised me by adding shutters outside the kitchen window. "Where did you learn to make shutters?" I asked, amazed that he would do this on his own initiative. He smiled shyly and looked away.

Did you go to school and learn to do carpentry work?" I pressed.

"No," he replied, glancing back at me. "I saw shutters on some houses in Popondetta, so I thought I would try making them for you."

"You mean these shutters are the first ones you ever made?" I asked incredulously, and watched his smile widen. His teeth gleamed. "Thank you!" I said with a new respect for this talented young man. "These are the best shutters in the country!"

With the help of the village children and other friends, we

33

moved into our new home. Every boy or girl who carried
a cardboard carton of supplies from Joshua's house to ours
received a few pieces of hard candy wrapped in colorful
cellophane paper. In less than twenty minutes every box
was moved and piled in our new living room. Glancing out
the window, I saw happy children sucking on their precious
candy. A piece of hard candy didn't seem like much, but to
these kids, it was like having a small chunk of the world.
There were no stores located nearby to purchase sweets of
any kind. Popondetta, the closest town, required a three-day
walk over steep mountains. Even so, once they arrived, where
would they get money to buy candy?

The back view of our new home that faces the mountains and gardens.

Every room in our new home had a view of the devastat-
ingly majestic mountains or the tumbling river below. My
study was spectacular. It was located in the far left-hand
corner of the house and I could see in two directions while
working at my desk. The view in front of me went down
the mountain to the river, and the view to the left took in

the sides of several mountains where gardens were planted. Then, in the far distance, I could see Onetaha, the tallest mountain on the horizon—the place where Rick, Randy and their friends hunted for birds and other wild animals. Memories flew to mind of the joyous looks on their faces when they came home with the animals they trapped on those mountains.

With all the grandeur of the Lord's creation outside my window, and the memories that went with them, would I ever get any work done?

"I remember the days of old; I meditate on all your works;
I ponder the work of Your hands." Psalm 143:5 (NKJV)

"'E'eju'e na tama veijija vwihajuta. 'Enarejo Ara iraka ka'ene maho'o vejajija majama hura hara vwihajuta. 'Ene Ara Oni iji kaukara ka'ene venajija vwihananamiuta." Samusi 143:5

Chapter 6

A Concern Too Small

The smell of new wood filled my nostrils as I unpacked cans of tuna and arranged them on a shelf in the pantry. How fortunate I felt to have a brand-new home with a place to put everything! Our village friends referred to the pantry as our "garden," because that was where we went to get our food.

Life was good, yet with each passing day, I sensed more and more the absence of our three children. My dry eyes filled whenever I thought about them. And, to make things worse, the people inquired everyday if Rick, Randy, or Tanya would ever come back. "Did they forget us?" they'd ask.

"No, they'll never forget you," I assured them, "but it takes a lot of money to buy a plane ticket. Maybe if they save enough money, they'll come," I said bleakly, not wanting to give them false hope.

Word about the financial need spread through the village. The following Tuesday at prayer meeting every woman asked God to give Rick, Randy and Tanya the money they would need to purchase plane tickets. And they prayed believing that He would.

One evening, ready to relax, I sat on the couch with a book by Corrie ten Boom. Soon after I opened the book, a sentence printed in quotes jumped out at me: *Any concern too small to be turned into a prayer is too small to be made into a burden.* Immediately, my thoughts flew back to the prayer meeting Jim and I had attended in a New York suburb in 1994. At that time, we were trying to raise our support level in order to return to Papua New Guinea.

Chairs, arranged in rows, filled the basement of the church. Pastor Dave Ballou stood behind a small pulpit at the front, ready to write down requests.

A middle-aged woman sitting across the aisle from us was the first to speak: "My cat Fudge is really sick," she lamented. "I don't know what to do for him. Please pray he'll get well."

I couldn't believe my ears—*asking prayer for a cat?* In our metropolitan church in New Jersey we didn't pray for cats or dogs. And if anyone had requested prayer for such, they would have been made a laughingstock.

My eyes flew from the woman to Pastor Dave. Surprised, I watched him calmly write down the woman's request as though it were nothing out of the ordinary. And when it came time to pray, he, himself, prayed for Fudge to get well. With one hand covering my mouth, I stifled the urge to snicker.

Now, two years later, sitting 13,000 miles away, I wondered what on earth prompted me to remember that night. The scene came vividly to mind, as though it were yesterday. Even the laughter I felt that evening mounted up inside me again.

I went back to ten Boom's book and re-read the quote, then waited for some visible dots to appear and connect the episode in New York with my life here in Numba Village.

None came.

A few days later, word got around that Mainare's cat had kittens. *A cat!* I thought: *With the kids now living in the states, it's the very thing we need here in the village!* Wasting no time, I made my way up into the village and down to the lower end where Mainare's house stood. The lady was Joshua's sister, like family to us.

"Jaki, choose any kitten you want," she urged.

As soon as I laid eyes on the all-black kitten, I knew he was the one. Gently, I lifted him from his bed and held him up for Mainare to see. She nodded her head. "Okay," she said approvingly, "but you have to wait till next week to take him — he's still nursing."

"Thank you," I said, and left her house feeling buoyant.

A few days later Mainare walked in the front door with the kitten in her arms. She noted the look of surprise on my face. "You have milk in your house," she explained, "so you can take your kitten now."

"Thank you," I said happily, and wondered what I could give her in exchange. Even though the law was not written in black and white, in this culture it was expected to give some form of payment for any gift.

"We don't have any kerosene," she announced, as though she read my mind. "Our rice is gone, and the family is hungry. My youngest doesn't have a blanket and sleeps cold every night …."

It wasn't hard to pour all my affection onto this kitten, and I never minded getting up in the middle of the night to feed him warm milk with an eyedropper. *Swahili*, we named him, after the name of a language in Africa where we had visited on our trip back to PNG. Cuddling the ball of black fur on my lap, I talked to him as though he were a person. Soon Swahili became a family member.

One night a few months later, Swahili didn't come home. Frantic and heartsick, I walked halfway down to the river, yelling his name into the night air. When the sound of rushing water below drowned out my voice, I knew it was useless to go any further. Devastated, I turned around and started back. I was halfway up the trail when about 12 or so village kids came running down to meet me.

"What's wrong?" they asked, their eyes fastened anxiously on my face. "We heard you calling and came to help. What happened?"

"I can't find Swahili," I moaned. I noted the concern in their expressions, and an idea leaped to mind: "Whoever finds my cat and brings him home will get a reward," I announced. Their expressions changed from concern to hope. Then, not wasting a second, they took off in different directions yelling "Swahili! Swahili!"

I turned around and started back up the trail. When I reached the top of the mountain, Pupudi appeared unexpectedly from out of the shadows. She listened to my tale of woe and shook her head. "Probably one of those rascal teenagers caught him, then roasted and ate him," she replied. My heart stopped beating.

"But my cat's not a bird or a flying fox," I pointed out, the tremor in my voice unmistakable.

"Years ago," she continued, speaking quietly in a doom-impending voice that scared me like nothing else could have, "when you and Jim were first living here with us, we used to eat only the wild pigs that lived in the jungle. But now all the pigs have been eaten. There's hardly any birds left either.

Everybody's hungry for meat. That's why the people eat cats now … and they say that cat's meat is very sweet."

Suddenly, I had a hard time breathing. Flicking on my flashlight, I turned and left Pupudi standing there without even saying goodbye. Overwrought, I searched around the outside of the house and in the brush that separated our house from the village. Then, in the moonlight, I saw Jim's figure moving towards the generator shed; it was time to shut down the generator and go to bed. He heard me yelling for the cat like a crazed person and said, "There's nothing more you can do tonight, so forget it and get some sleep."

I nodded, resigned. Still, there was something about Jim's complacence that annoyed me. How could he treat the matter so lightly while it was eating me up alive? Still, he was right—I had done everything possible. Reluctantly, I gave up the search and went inside to get ready for bed.

After the drone of the generator died, the chirping of crickets filled the air like a symphony that I was not in the mood to listen to. In the pitch black of night, I lay on the bed aching for my cat with thoughts of how he might have died rolling around in my head: *How did those boys kill him? Did they hit him on the head with a rock and slit his throat like they killed pigs? Did they boil him? Or roast him over hot coals?*

Suddenly, from out of nowhere, thoughts of the lady in the rural New York church asking prayer for her cat came to mind. *Could this be the reason I remembered the incident so vividly that night? Was God preparing me back then to now face this moment?*

I had laughed at that woman, now I was in the same situation—sick with worry for my cat, desperate to know the outcome, and only God could help.

"Lord," I prayed, "You know where Swahili is. If he's alive, please send him home soon."

Opening my eyes, I wondered if God had really heard me. Was a nobody like me worthy to speak to Almighty God about such a trite concern? With wars going on and people starving in other countries, this was definitely a "concern too small." Yet, my cat was, to me, a concern too big.

Still hanging onto my burden, I lay in the darkness, my mind holding me prisoner. I listened to Jim's steady breathing. He was sound asleep. "There's nothing you can do about it," he had said simply, and fallen off to sleep.

Jim truly believed that no matter what happened in our lives, God would take care of it. That belief enabled him to sleep without a care in the world.

I'd often heard other people say "Let go and let God." At this moment, I wished I could do just that. But where would I get the power? How do I start?

Lord, teach me how.

As I uttered those words, I knew in my heart that I had to pray again and, somehow, leave the cat totally in God's hands.

"Thank You for teaching me this lesson about praying for animals," I began weakly. "*Now* I know I shouldn't have laughed at that woman's request. *Now* I understand.

"Lord, I don't know if I have the right to ask for this, but my heart is on my cat, and I'd really like You to send him home to me. You already know how much I want Swahili to come back. But … if You have other plans, I'm ready to receive it. You alone know what's best for me, so if the cat is dead, it's okay. I give You the whole burden. Please take it, Lord. Thank You."

Ahh, peace at last. I knew it was God Who gave me the strength to give Him my problem and let go of it. And now that the cat no longer seemed so all-important, so all-encompassing, I had peace. In fact, I felt like I was floating.

Just on the edge of sleep, I heard a faint whimpering sound

at the bottom of our bed. Then, I felt a light pressure pulling the covers. Next, the pressure came creeping up on the bed towards my head. I was holding my breath when the loud purring began.

"Jim!" I yelled, shaking him. "Swahili's back! He's alive!"

"Huh?" he groaned.

"God heard my cries and sent Swahili home. Listen to him purring!"

"Mmm, yeah, that's good," he said in a sleepy voice and rolled over, then firmly placed the pillow over his ear.

I began kissing my cat on the top of his head. "Where were you?" I scolded, and kissed him again. Cuddling him under my armpit, I lay stretched out on the bed feeling ecstatic that God should answer my "small" concern.

"Thank You, Jesus!" I said exuberantly over and over. "In the midst of war and starvation, You thought about me and my cat."

That God cared about the small matters in my life was an amazing discovery. Swahili was important to God, too.

Because the cat was important to me.

"When I am afraid, I will trust in You. In God, whose word I praise, in God I trust; I will not be afraid..." Psalm 56:3–4 (NIV)

"Vea ka'ene na juvujaho na A nimaa vetaura. 'Ene na Godiho nimaa vetihu jihuna'e Huni irijaho na 'aromahuna. 'Ene emaa haha rukina iraka nununa'i ve'eja? Na niho'o paju'eju." Samusi 56:3–4

Chapter 7

Faith Becomes Sight

Although Jim and I enjoyed living in our new home, not having running water in the house was a hardship. We needed water to cook, take showers, and, most importantly, to drink. Some of the older children went down to the river every day after school with buckets to fetch the much-needed water for us. Still, if only we could buy a tank to collect rain water from the roof, our problem would be solved. Building the house, however, had depleted our funds and, therefore, we had no money to make a trip to Popondetta to buy the tank.

Pilot Steve Baptista and his family would be arriving soon to spend the Christmas holidays with us in the village. Thoughts of having no indoor water weighed heavily on my mind. Steve and his wife, Sarah, had five children, their youngest not yet walking. The rainy season also meant the muddy season. How would we keep the children clean without running water in the house?

Over lunch I voiced my concern to Jim.

Jim replied: "There's an old fiberglass tank lying in two pieces under Pastor Ivan's house. I think I could probably fix it up."

"Really?" I managed to ask, my hopes mounting.

"I was looking at it the other day," Jim continued. "All it needs is a good cleaning out, a few bolts and some sealer."

"Do you have bolts that would fit?"

"Probably."

"And sealer?"

"I think so. I'll have to look around in the storeroom to see what I've got. But first I better see what Ivan plans to do with the tank."

"Right," I agreed as Jim drained the last of his iced tea. Then he pushed back from the table and went over to Ivan's house. A few minutes later he came back, Pastor Ivan trailing a few feet behind, each carrying half of the fiberglass tank. Ivan saw me through the kitchen window and smiled. "We weren't going to use it anyway," he said, "so you can have it."

"Thank you!" I replied ecstatically. With Jim's skills, I knew he'd have the tank together in no time. Soon there would be running water in the house! This meant no more trips to the river to haul water, no more boiling it for safe drinking, no more worrying about keeping the Baptista kids clean. My spirits soared. "Yay! Hooray!" I yelled, as if I were back in the Yankee Stadium.

Jim worked for two days sanding the tank, then scrubbing it with a scrub brush. Next he applied sealer to both rims and pressed them together so that the tank was in one piece.

After tightening the bolts, several men helped lift the tank onto the stand. Jim then attached the downspout from the gutter into the tank. "All we need now is rain," he remarked and looked across the valley toward the mountains. Dark clouds were moving in; a storm was brewing.

That night, after we had gone to bed, lightning flashed, thunder roared, and rain pelted down on our tin roof. "That downpour should fill our tank in about an hour or two," Jim assured me.

I went to sleep with a smile on my face.

I awoke at three in the morning. The rain had subsided.

Would there be running water when I turned on the tap? I had to get out of bed and check.

Gingerly, I sat up, felt around for my flashlight, got up and tiptoed down the hall to the kitchen. I held my breath and turned on the tap. Lo and behold, water spilled out plentifully into the sink. What a beautiful sight!

"Thank You, Lord," I whispered. "Thank You for supplying us with water — water we thought would be impossible to have so soon." I ran back to the bedroom to wake Jim with the good news.

The next day I decided to bake cookies to offer the Baptistas when they arrived in a few days. As I reached for my cookbook, I heard a loud noise outside — like a bomb exploding.

What was that? I thought with alarm. Suddenly the house rocked violently. *We're having an earthquake,* I concluded, and grabbed onto the counter for support as the house continued to sway. When, at last the movement slowed, a disheartening groan came from out on the porch.

Fear hurled me out the door to find Jim and Isoro standing there staring wide-eyed at the ground, their mouths open. I jerked my head around to see what they were gaping at. There, on the ground beside the house lay our gleaming, bleach-scrubbed tank in three pieces. It wasn't an earthquake at all, but it did look like a tornado had struck and scissored the tank into jagged sections. For a moment there was complete silence except for the sound of water gushing.

Jim and I exchanged glances, and I could read his eyes. He'd never seen anything worse. Helplessly the three of us looked on as water poured from the damaged tank, rushing under the house and finally down to the river below—all 1,000 gallons of it.

Jim stooped over to check under the house. "Good thing no kids were playing under there today," he remarked.

"If children were playing under the house, they would have died," Isoro finished. Lines of concern etched his forehead.

I didn't see Poki's son Luke coming through the brush that separated his brother's house from ours. Now he wore an anxious look as he approached us.

"Luke!" Jim yelled out to him. "Check and see if anyone was coming up the footpath from the river!" Jim directed.

A sense of dread filled me as I followed Jim and Isoro to the back of the house. We stood silently waiting at the top of the embankment where we could see Luke going down the footpath in soup-like mud, struggling to keep his balance.

"If any little kids were coming up the path, they would have been swept back down to the river and drowned," Jim said softly. "There's no way they could have stood up to the force of that much water; it would have hit them like a brick wall. Even adults wouldn't have had time to get out of the way."

I took a long, deep, prayer-filled breath. "Oh Lord, please don't let it be so."

Jim walked further down the muddy path, his eyes straining for some sign of Luke. At last, the lean form appeared scrambling back up the mucky footpath. "It's okay!" Luke shouted. "No one was going down to the river or coming up!" Relief flickered over Jim's face as he turned to go back to the scene of the crime. Numbly, I followed.

Crowds of people streamed from the village to our house.

Fifty or more waited by the damaged tank with awestruck looks. "What happened?" they asked, their foreheads wrinkled with concern.

Jim squatted down to examine the pieces of the tank more closely. "The fiberglass was just too old to stand the pressure of all the water," he explained.

Back in the house I sat on the couch and stared out the window with unseeing eyes. A vision of water being carried up the mountainside in countless buckets filled my mind. My mood sank. "Lord, why did You allow this to happen? Did You lift me up to the sky this morning only to send me plummeting back down again? You could have at least waited until the Baptista family went back to Ukarumpa before allowing this to happen!"

As I sat pondering the events, Jim's words floated to mind — *the fiberglass was too old*. I got up and reached for my Bible. Flipping through the first few pages of Matthew I immediately found what I was searching for: *And no one puts new wine into old wineskins. For the old skins would burst from the pressure, spilling the wine and ruining the skins."* Matthew 9:17

There's where we made our mistake — taking an old tank and putting in fresh (new) water; it burst from the pressure and ruined the tank. Now we were back to square one — sending the school children to carry water by the bucket, then boiling the drinking water. A family with five small children meant a lot of water for washing and a lot to boil for drinking.

Sleep did not come easily that night. *How would we get money to buy "new skins"?* I wondered, tossing and turning. Even if we did get enough money, there wouldn't be time to go to Popondetta, buy a tank, hire a vehicle, and drive it back to Numba. Besides, what driver would be willing to drive over these mountains during the rainy season? Trucks never came to our village during the rainy season, the roads are just too muddy. All was lost now, I concluded, and sank into a valley of despair.

I lay in bed listening to the roosters crowing, first one just outside the window, then another closer to the church building. They crowed back and forth as though they were carrying on a conversation. It seemed like dawn would never come. Finally, a little after five, I heard voices muttering outside on the porch.

"Who's there?" I called out, waking Jim.

"It's us," a few voices replied simultaneously.

I threw on my robe and pushed my feet into flip-flops. "I'll go see what they want," I said to Jim and scurried down the hall through the kitchen to the porch. Upon opening the door, I saw several men with money in their hands. Poki, Jim's former translation helper, was among them. Some held 100-kina notes, some 50. When Jim joined me, the men promptly handed him their bills. "What's this for?" he asked, looking to each man, then settling his eyes on Poki.

"We feel sorry about what happened to your tank," Poki explained, "so we want to help you buy a new one."

"But we don't know when we'll be able to pay you back," I blurted out. "It could be a long time."

"That's okay. Some day you'll have money and can pay us back then."

Staring at the men, I hoped the love I felt for each of them would reach out so they could feel it, too.

Jim counted all the bills. "There's enough to buy a tank," he said, looking at me as if to ask, "What should we do?"

Poki broke in: "Give me the money! I'll walk to Afore, wait for a truck and go to Popondetta. After I buy the tank, I'll look for another truck to bring me back."

Murmurs of assent and nods came from the others, urging Jim to send Poki.

Jim looked at Poki and shook his head. "How will you get a truck at Afore? No trucks will be able to drive that far over these swampy roads."

"Yes, Afore is a government station and government vehicles will come," Poki countered. "I'll just go and wait."

Poki's trip meant a two-hour walk to the government station, probably in the pouring rain. Then, if a truck happened to come, it would be a five-hour drive to town. *Impossible!* Yet, Poki's courage humbled me, and I stared at him through new eyes. "You might be wasting your time," I said slowly. "Are you *sure* you want to do this?"

"Of course!" Poki replied without hesitation. "You're *my family*. I want to help you!" His look was serious, and his words struck deep.

"Another thing," Poki added, his excitement growing. "I know the store owner, he'll help me."

Even though his enthusiastic words encouraged me, I refused to hope. I definitely did not want my spirits to come plummeting down a second time.

"What have we got to lose?" Jim asked me, and handed the 700 kina to Poki.

"I'll write down the type of tank I want," he told Poki. "If your friend doesn't sell this type, get the nearest thing to it."

Later that morning some of the women stopped by on their way to church for a special prayer meeting. "We're

going to ask God to help Poki get a truck to town," Pupudi
said from outside the kitchen window. Poki was Pupudi's
brother. "God can help him find a tank and bring him back
this afternoon. Do you want to come and pray with us?"
she invited. Her eyes stayed fixed on me as she waited for
my answer.

Caught off guard, I fumbled for the right words. "Err, not
right now," I stammered. "Maybe when I finish baking …."

"Okay, just come when you can," Pupudi replied and trotted off towards the church with the other women.

The odds were 99 to 1 against Poki finding a truck to
take him to Popondetta, then another to bring him back
with our water tank. I stood on the porch a few minutes
listening to them pray. Each voice prayed earnestly for Poki's
safe return to the village with the tank. And they prayed
believing, thanking the Lord as though Poki were already
back with the tank.

I listened to the eagerness in their tone. They weren't
worrying about the rain or muddy roads, but they had complete peace as they talked to God and sang hymns of praise
to Him. It occurred to me that these women had their faith
and joy rooted in Jesus, not in circumstances.

But in my heart, down deep where the truth stayed hidden,
I knew I wouldn't be going to pray with them. I was disappointed in God and didn't want to talk to Him right then.

Hours later, about 5:00 in the afternoon I heard shouting:
"A truck is coming! A truck is coming!"

"*No way!*" I thought, racing out to the porch. Sure enough,
the far-off sound of an engine pierced through the fog
and drizzle. After praying all day, the ladies scurried from
the church looking like they would burst with happiness.
Trying to contain myself, I walked over to join them in the
churchyard.

Like an army tank cutting its way through a jungle, the front fender of a grey truck pushed its way through the hedge that fenced in the church center. The women let out a whooping cheer. They began hugging one another with tears of joy. *Their faith had become sight!* I pinched my arm to make sure I wasn't dreaming. My thoughts turned to God: *Despite my lack of faith and unchristian example to the women, He allowed me to see this miracle.*

Poki and the driver got out to unload the tank. Promptly, Jim began to help. He then motioned to some men who were standing by gawking, and they jumped into action. About 15 able-bodied men helped Jim lug the tank over to our house. There they hoisted it up onto the tank stand, and Jim made the proper connections from the drain pipe to the new tank. It didn't take long, and the tank was ready to collect rainwater. What God had just given us was better than what I had hoped for in the beginning of our tank experience.

"Thank You, Lord, for not putting me away on a shelf when I refused to believe," I prayed silently. "When it seemed safer to doubt and remain aloof, You didn't punish me, but remained faithful."

O the deep, deep love of Jesus, vast, unchanging like the sea.

When Steve and Sarah arrived with their children the next day, the tank was half full, which meant there was plenty of water for all our needs. Seeing friends from Ukarumpa filled me with indescribable happiness. How proud I felt to show them our new home and offer them a cold drink from our

kerosene-run refrigerator. The chocolate chip cookies I baked
on the day of the disaster disappeared in a hurry.

The red mailbag lay on the table and, while the Baptistas
unpacked, I stole away to read the mail. Anxious for news
from home, I tore into the letters. One bore the name "Bailey."
Max was in our wedding party 38 years ago. Both he and
his wife Joanne were dear friends. I quickly ripped open the
envelope. A check for $500 dropped out—the equivalent
of 1,500 kina. The amount was more than twice what we
paid for the tank!

The Lord had taken care of every detail concerning the
water tank. Would I remember this miracle the next time
a crisis arose? Would I trust Him then? I hoped so, but if
I didn't, I knew His forgiveness would be there for me again.
And again the next time.

And for always.

---

*"The Lord is compassionate and gracious, slow to anger,
abounding in love." Psalm 103:8 (NIV)*

"Na Oni varapijija 'ajohe vehune. Enakune pamaho'o makima
paranana." Samusi 103:8

Chapter 8

The First Christmas Pageant

Although the Managalasi people knew the Christmas story well, they had never seen a Christmas pageant. Drama wasn't new to this culture; the men loved to dress up with elaborate headdresses, retrieve the old wooden shields stored in the rafters of their houses and re-enact scenes from long-ago tribal warfare days.

Another favorite to re-enact was impersonating the first white man who came to their village and ordered them to stop killing. This government man, known to them as Misimatoia, took their spears and broke them over his knee. Then he shook his head from side to side to communicate *no more fighting!*

Acting out historical events was a pertinent and enjoyable way of passing along information to descendants. Being an oral culture, they used this method for generations. The village people loved to watch these performances and thereby learn their history.

Christmas would be coming soon, just a few weeks left. "It's time for them to see a Christmas pageant," I determined, and flipped through my Bible to the Christmas story in Luke's Gospel. As I read over the account of Christ's birth, visions of scenes for the manger, the shepherds, King Herod and the wise men flashed vividly in my mind. I sat down at my computer and made a list of all the characters involved. Next, I typed out speaking parts for each character. Excitement mounted, and in my heart I knew this would be a memorable event for them. *I'll announce it at the conclusion of Tuesday's prayer meeting,* I decided.

The following Tuesday morning, after the final prayer was uttered, I stood up quickly and cleared my throat noisily to get everyone's attention. "We're going to have a Christmas pageant," I announced boldly. Heads jerked in my direction as I made my way to the front. The women studied me through quizzical eyes and waited to hear more.

Without wasting a second, I plunged right in. "This Christmas we're going to act out the story of Jesus' birth. We'll invite other villages to come and watch the pageant with us."

The air grew electric. "What?" several asked simultaneously, looking at each other, then back to me. Chipi, Pastor Ivan's wife, had participated in plays before and knew exactly what I was talking about. I asked her to explain my plan to the women in clear Managalasi talk so they would understand in detail.

Chipi stood up promptly and explained about the Christmas pageant. When the event became clear in their minds, they all began talking at once. As they chattered, an enthusiastic spirit pervaded. Their reaction proved to me that they were excited about the idea and would enjoy doing the pageant.

Utu, one of the younger women, sat quietly on the bench taking in all the chatter. One quick glance at her and I knew she would be a perfect Mary.

"Okay!" I yelled loudly above their animated talk, signaling that I needed their attention once again. Looking directly at my choice to play the mother of Jesus, I asked: "Utu, would you be Mary in the pageant?"

The shy girl, taken by surprise, looked down quickly at her lap without replying.

"Samai could be Joseph," I pushed, knowing that if her husband were in the play, she'd be more accepting. "And your baby could be Jesus!" I finished brightly.

Utu thought about being a main character in the play and allowed a thin line of a smile as she looked up at me. Slowly, she nodded her consent. Then, to hide her embarrassment, covered her face with both hands.

"Thank you," I acknowledged, and turned to face the group. "I need three of you to be shepherds; if you can read your language, raise your hand!" All but a few raised their hands.

As my eyes fell over their animated faces, I spotted two with loud voices who weren't shy. Pastor Ivan's wife was one. "Chipi, would you like to be a shepherd?" I asked. The pastor's wife looked away, feigning a shyness I knew was not there. Yet, it was the customary way to behave so as to play down special favor shown. The room grew silent. "If you would rather not, that's okay," I assured her. Then, from out of the silence came the "yes" I expected.

"Thank you," I said, and turned to another young mother who was not shy and spoke with a loud voice. "Damaris, would you like to be a shepherd?"

"Yes," she replied confidently.

The women seemed happy with the casting so far and continued talking animatedly, speculating on who the third shepherd might be. I noticed Kristoni staring up at me, her eyes begging. She was much older than the other women, but had learned to read her language well. *Why not?* I thought. "Kristoni, will you be the third shepherd?" I asked. Instantly the room grew silent—my first clue that perhaps I had made the wrong choice.

Nevertheless, Kristoni's eyes shone brighter than ever. "Yes," she blurted out and looked around proudly at the others.

There was a low murmur, and I examined the faces of the women who stared back at me clearly unimpressed. The silence that followed made it obvious I had made a dreadful mistake. I swallowed hard and cleared my throat.

"Okay, shepherds," I said, trying to ignore the negative feeling closing in over me. "Come back tonight at seven and we'll go over your parts together. The rest of you will be angels and sing a Christmas song. Think about how you will dress to look like angels."

The last announcement set the chatter going wildly again, and I felt better.

That evening at practice with the shepherds, Chipi and Damaris read their parts well and understood exactly what was happening. Kristoni, however, seemed confused, and when it was her time to speak, seemed paralyzed with fear.

Instead of moving onward, she read the very same line over and over. I wondered what was going on in her head.

"You're not thinking!" Damaris rebuked unkindly. I saw anger on her face. "You already said that! Don't keep saying the same thing over and over! Say the next line!"

Looking to Chipi I noted that her eyes widened. In this culture you don't show disrespect to an older person. Kristoni didn't say a word. She couldn't even look at Damaris. Or me. Her head was down, her eyes trained on the dirt floor of the church. Had we started a process that could go long into the night?

Kristoni's problem set the three of us on edge, stretching us to the limit. The older lady couldn't remember when it was her time to speak or what she was supposed to say. As if in a daze, Kristoni would wait for one of us to shout her name before responding. There was no doubt about it, Kristoni was hopeless.

The clock was ticking, and we didn't have time to waste. After the other two shepherds went home, I stayed behind to help Kristoni go over her lines again. "Pretend I'm the angel who appears before you on the mountain," I instructed and stood in front of her with my arms stretched out like wings. Kristoni stared back at me, clueless.

"Act like you're afraid," I prompted. "Then say your line!"

A look of fright came over her, and she stood as rigid as a board. *Was she going to have a stroke?* I wondered with alarm. Instinctively, I touched her shoulder to reassure her as if she were a child. "What are the first words you're going to say?" I probed.

"I don't know," she whimpered, and covered her face with both hands.

Discouraged but not deterred, I exhibited a patience I didn't know I possessed. "Repeat these words after me," I said softly and put my arm around her shoulders. We went through all three lines thoroughly again and again. Still, a thickness seemed to block her thinking. She was never sure of herself. Then an idea came: *I'll give Chipi one of her lines to speak. That should take care of the problem.*

Still, it took going through the scene 12 times before Kristoni could say both lines correctly. Mercifully, it was time to call it a day, and I told Kristoni to go home and sleep well.

Bone tired, I staggered home. *I really don't want to do this,* I thought, *especially while the Baptistas are visiting.* Yet, because my objective pulled so strongly on my heartstrings, I knew I would endure anything to see it happen. My objective being that the Managalasi people see the Christmas pageant and learn more of what actually happened in Bethlehem the night the Son of God came to earth and was born in a stable.

The next morning, feeling thankful to have Sarah there, I talked over my frustration with her. She looked at me thoughtfully. "It seems to me that Kristoni was chosen for a special purpose," she replied, then stood up and walked to the kitchen window. "You know what I think?" she asked, staring thoughtfully out the window. Then, without waiting for my response, she said: "I don't think you made a mistake when you chose Kristoni. I feel that it's God's plan for her to be one of the shepherds. Maybe we'll see the reason why before the pageant's over, and maybe we won't. But one thing for sure is that you aren't wasting time by helping her."

As I sat processing Sarah's words, she abruptly changed the subject. "How much do you think that stalk of bananas weighs?" she asked.

Quickly I got up and joined her at the window. Outside, Pastor Michael struggled up the mountain balancing a stalk of almost-ripe bananas on his shoulder. "Probably about 90 pounds," I replied.

A stalk of bananas, usually weighing about 80 lbs., is balanced on the shoulder when carried.

"Wow," she gasped, as though it were a two-syllable word.

As I watched Pastor Michael wobble past the window towards his house, an idea struck. "Aparihi!" I yelled, using the name his mother had given him at birth. He turned to look in my direction. "Wait!" I called, and rushed out onto the porch. Not wasting a second, I blurted out what had come to mind. "There are no Christmas songs written in our language and we need one right away. Would you write one the women could sing for our Christmas pageant?"

I held my breath as he bent forward to unload the burden from his shoulder. He was laughing as he leaned the bananas against our garden fence and came to join me on the porch. "What did you say?" he asked, still smiling.

I repeated my request. Unlike me, Aparihi was not one to make rash decisions. Right away his face grew serious and he sat down on the bamboo bench to think about what I was asking. When he didn't answer right away, I continued.

"The women will go to the front of the church and sing your new song while the scenery is being changed. You would just have to compose a melody to go along with some words about Jesus coming to earth as a baby. Look in Luke, chapter 2, for the words to use, then compose a melody to go with them.

"Just think," I added lightly, as though the enormous thing I was requesting was an ordinary occurrence. "This will be our first Christmas song composed in the Managalasi language. Won't that be wonderful?"

I hoped my enthusiasm would create an insatiable desire in him to compose the song, but that wasn't Aparihi's style. Instead, he pondered my words for a long time without saying a word.

"What do you think?" I pushed, forcing him to speak. "Would you be able to compose a song we can use this Christmas?" My stomach churned as I waited for his reply. If Aparihi refused, the women would have to learn a Christmas carol in the English language. Over half of them couldn't speak a word of it.

"I'll try," he said at last, and stood to go. "But Jaki, I can't promise you it will be good."

Relief spread through me from head to toe. "Don't worry about whether it will be good or not. God will give you a melody, just ask Him."

Aparihi left the porch with an uncertain look and returned to his banana stalk. He bent low so the bananas would fall onto his shoulder in just the right spot. Then he lifted the stalk and started down the path towards his house.

"Oh, one more thing!" I called out recklessly, knowing full well I would be asking for the moon this time. "Can you have the song ready by next Tuesday's prayer meeting?...and come and teach it to the ladies after our prayer meeting?"

A guffaw burst from his throat as he turned his head towards me. "I'll let you know," he promised graciously, and wobbled beneath his heavy burden, balancing the stalk as best he could.

I went back into the kitchen. Sarah had started making flour tortillas, and I knew we were in for a treat at supper-time. I told her about the conversation between Aparihi and me. Her eyes widened. "You mean Pastor Michael can write music, too?"

"Oh, sure," I said. "There are a few men in our village who write songs. That's how we got our hymnbook."

"But who taught them how to compose songs?"

"No one. It's a gift from God."

Chululu was the best public reader in the village, and I asked him to narrate the Christmas program. I handed him the script which consisted mostly of Scripture verses. He took it eagerly and began reading in a loud, commanding voice. *He'll be fantastic,* I thought.

Next I chose Ahause, Chululu's son, to play King Herod. I watched Ahause during practices. Without any coaching, he used all the right gestures to portray a contemptible king. *With such natural talent, this guy could have easily been a Hollywood star*, I marveled.

The three wise men would be enacted by Kwaare, Alfred and Jiveta. Practicing with them and King Herod was a breeze in comparison to practicing with the shepherds. Little effort was required and, after going over their parts only once, they took it from there like experienced actors, improvising as they saw fit.

During one practice, the wise men left King Herod standing arrogantly with his arms folded across his chest. Then, in their own creative way, the three men portrayed traveling over a long, hard road by winding up and down the church aisles. Finally, they settled on a spot in the front where they would "spend the night."

The wise men removed woven mats from their backpacks, spread them out flat on the dirt floor at the front of the church and lay down. Suddenly Kwaare sat up, grabbed his backpack, and took out a flashlight. I felt my mouth drop open. Next, he brought out three cooked ears of corn and passed them to his buddies. "Here," he told them, "you must be hungry." The other two grunted and reached for the corn. Next, out came a cucumber, and the three of them munched away. I couldn't believe what I was seeing. This was *not* in the script.

After eating, the three wise men lay back down, only to toss and turn on their mats. Finally, when they quieted down, Jiveta complained of being cold. Alfred took out a box of matches, lit one and put it next to the complainer's feet. This was the signal for Kwaare to begin twitching and kicking at invisible mosquitoes.

Where did they come up with all this added drama? I wondered in utter disbelief. Then it dawned on me: this is the way these three men perceived how the event had occurred — the wise men would be hungry after travelling and likely feel cold in the night air without a fire. Their perceptions could be right on.

I marveled at their creativity, yet sat with baited breath hoping their shenanigans would come to an end soon. They did, and shortly after that scene, the three of them were out on the road again, heading for the manger scene.

At home Jim and Steve used aluminum foil to hand-craft a large star and took it to the church. The wise men followed the improvised star from the back entrance to the manger at the front. When the men arrived at the manger, they presented baby Jesus with gifts of gold, frankincense and myrrh. Their performance filled me with awe.

Practice took place every evening until the night of the final performance. The practices were not without problems. For one thing, very few village people owned watches. Not being a time-oriented culture, no one arrived on time. These Managalasi people did not see the need to hurry to the river for a bath nor hurry to eat so they wouldn't be late. The scheduled seven o'clock practices often began at nine or later. *Life would be so much easier without the worry of the pageant,* I thought, and the temptation to quit haunted me daily.

The worst problem was the village children who showed up every night to watch "the show." They had no TV to watch, no games to play, no books at home to read. Coming to rehearsals was an entertaining way to spend an otherwise uneventful evening. Not that they cared about the story taking place, they came to have a rip-roaring good time. Every word uttered on stage was hilarious to them, and their piercing outbursts put me on edge. When their noise grew deafening, I knew something had to be done.

"Okay, kids, you have to leave!" I ordered.

The kids, vibrant and aimless, mumbled in the back rows

of the church. I doubt it was flattering talk. "You're making too much noise," I pointed out, using a softer tone. "I can't hear what's being said on stage, so please go outside."

Eyes filled with laughter blinked back at me. No one attempted to leave.

This reaction presented another worry to my already stress-racked head. How was I going to get these noisy, hyper kids out of the auditorium? I rubbed circles on my throbbing temples with my thumbs. "Lord, what should I do?" I prayed, at which moment Chululu walked into the church. Heads turned back to see him. The kids were suddenly in a state of high alert. From the disturbed look on Chululu's face, I knew he had heard what I said to the children.

He came to my side and, without wasting a moment, addressed the four rows of children: "All you kids get up and go outside *now!*"

One look from him settled it quickly. Immediately, the kids scattered like cockroaches in all directions: "When Jaki tells you to do something, you do it!" he called out after them. A flash of anger went through him before he added: "Don't come back unless Jaki says it's all right for you to come!"

I closed my eyes and let loose a satisfying sigh. What a difference the quiet atmosphere made to the performance, the participants, and to my sanity.

The village buzzed. Volunteers went out readily into the deepest part of the jungle and cut down the materials needed to build a manger. Isoro's son happily took the poster paper

I gave him to draw donkeys, cows and lambs that would form the background to the manger. Others cut poinsettias and decorated both entranceways into the church. Leafy vines wound around all the poles inside the building. Enthusiasm spread to a feverish pitch. *The spirit of Christmas in Numba Village is what it should be the world over,* I reflected, despite the stress producing the pageant brought me.

The women were faithful to attend every rehearsal to learn Pastor Michael's new song. As I expected, the song was perfect. I knew God had given Michael the melody.

Pastor Jethro's wife had the voice of an angel and led the singing boldly from her place in line. Their efforts during practices never failed to draw adults from the village to the church to peer through the windows and enjoy the beautiful music.

Mary, Pastor Jethro's wife, equipped with a beautiful voice, often leads the women in singing.

Jim and Steve's hand-made star was fastened to a small lantern and rigged up onto a long wire to be pulled along gently for the wise men to follow to the manger. The Lord provided all the skills necessary to pull off the production. The most awesome wonder of all was that I, with no training or experience, was the director of the play.

Was this being all things to all men? I didn't know, but I saw that it was God alone who did the enabling.

The pageant was scheduled to begin at 7:30 on Christmas Eve. Jim and I arranged to go caroling in the village with Steve and his family around 4:00. Then, after singing a Christmas carol in English, we planned to personally invite the families to attend the pageant. Steve brought along his guitar from Ukarumpa. I was thankful for his accompaniment which enabled us to sing the carols on key.

Hearing carolers sing was a first for Numba Village. As we approached the doorways, the families seemed startled to see us. Immediately, we began singing. Some young people who were familiar with the carol sang along with us. After the first few phrases, the people sat back and relaxed, their puzzled expressions replaced with admiring glances, especially toward Steve and Sarah's children. Those five kids had stolen their hearts.

Before moving on to the next house, we invited each family to the pageant, even though we knew that a downpour of hailstones the size of boulders wouldn't keep them away. By the time we finished caroling, families from the surrounding villages were beginning to arrive. Thanks to the effective grapevine, more and more people from far-away villages came pouring into Numba Village to see the pageant.

Sarah's homemade bread made our light supper special that night. The clock struck six—just an hour and a half to go. As we sat eating, a faint knock came on the door. I glanced up to see Alfred, one of the wise men, standing in the doorway. "Can I borrow one of Jim's shirts for tonight?" he asked slowly, his voice nervous and at least an octive higher than normal. "One that has long sleeves," he added. His voice actually shook a bit when he explained why: "I don't want my arms to show."

"Jim doesn't have any shirts with long sleeves," I answered truthfully, "but I have a housecoat with long sleeves."

Alfred looked doubtful. Without waiting for his reply, I got my housecoat and slipped it over his head before he got the chance to see what it looked like. He proceeded to stretch out his arms; the sleeves were exactly the right length. He looked at me and nodded his head up and down a few times. "Okay," he said, and left with a smile.

The church was jam-packed and overflowing, producing a new experience of the jitters for me. I could count on one hand how many times I'd ever directed a pageant before, and I'd still have five fingers left over. *Don't worry, Jaki,* I told myself. *After tonight you'll be able to say you're an experienced Director.*

Once again, Chululu ordered the children to go outside in order to make room for the adults who had come from other villages. I sat down on the front bench and went over the script one last time. Thoughts of Kristoni mixing up her lines filled me with anxiety. I was beyond thinking, took a deep breath and waited in dismal anticipation.

At 7:45 Pastor Michael stood and led the crowd in singing a familiar Managalasi hymn. At the conclusion, he gave me a nod. I stood quickly and turned to face the tremendous crowd. My spine prickled as all heads swiveled in my direction. The audience, packed to the walls, grew stone silent as I delivered my welcome speech and introduction to the pageant. They watched every turn of my head and focused on my every word. My knees were putty. I was sweating. When I finished speaking, I signaled Chululu to begin reading the narration.

As he read the familiar passage, Utu and Samai made their trek down the aisle as Mary and Joseph. Mary held her baby wrapped securely in a blanket, and they took their places inside the manger scene. Everything was running smoothly so far.

Chululu continued reading as the shepherds, pretending to feed their sheep, approached the stage making wide, sweeping motions with their arms as if scattering seeds. When the time came for Kristoni to utter her first line, I again felt perspiration forming at my hairline. She spoke her first words, and I gasped — those words were *not* what I had written for her to say. Yet, she said what needed to be said using her own words. My fear turned to awe as I gazed around at the audience to check their reaction. The effect was powerful. And Kristoni needed no prompting which, to my mind, was miraculous.

Now it was time for the angels to make their appearance. Several wore white blouses. Some draped white towels around their shoulders. Two wrapped white sheets that covered their entire bodies. Mary gave the signal with a nod of her head, and they stood to their feet. As they moved to the front of the church, they began singing Aparihi's version of "Glory to God in the Highest." Each woman held a bouquet of long-stemmed flowers. Their voices rose in song, echoing through the heavy night air. As they sang the last verse, they simultaneously raised the flowers high above their heads and waved them back and forth in adoration to the new-born King. The effect was sensational. *This is the closest thing to a Broadway production the Managalasis will ever see,* I thought in awe.

When King Herod took the stage, you could have heard a chicken feather drop. The audience, not wanting to miss one gesture, sat transfixed on the edge of their seats. I gazed at the enraptured faces around me and sent a silent prayer of thanks to God, grateful that this group of people could not only see the Christmas story performed, but hear the words being spoken in their own language.

When the three wise men entered, I took one look at Alfred and thought my eyes would pop from their sockets. The man had wound two cloths around the top of his head and fastened a baby blanket on top. Beneath my housecoat he wore two shirts, his wife's dress and a skirt. He looked ready for the snows of Mt. Kilimanjaro.

The conversation with King Herod and the wise men went perfectly. Later, after the three men reached their camp site, Alfred pulled out his flashlight and brought the house down with laughter. Even this unschooled audience knew that two millennia ago, there were no flashlights.

Eventually, it came time to follow the star to the manger where they presented their gifts to the baby Jesus. When the scene ended, silence filled the room. No one in the audience moved. Instead, they sat staring straight ahead as if trying to store in their minds forever the things they had seen and heard. I let the silence linger so the audience could savor this night and this moment a little longer.

Turning around I saw Pastor Jethro standing at the side of the building leaning against the wall unashamedly wiping tears from his cheeks. Touched by his response, I stood up, wordlessly announcing that the pageant had ended and it was time to leave.

I made my way over to Jethro, one of the assistant pastors. "Did you enjoy the play?" I asked, and watched him swallow hard as if words wanted to come, but couldn't. The pastor closed his eyes and let loose a deep, satisfying sigh. He grasped my hand, shaking his head from side to side. "The play was wonderful," he said finally. "Even though I read the Christmas story many times and taught about the birth of Christ year after year, tonight was like hearing it for the first time."

I felt warm tears sliding out of the corners of my eyes as I nodded back at him. "Good, I'm glad you liked it," I managed to say, afraid my voice would crack. The lump in my throat stayed with me as I turned away from him and maneuvered through the crowd to the back of the church where thicker crowds were exiting. Some adults saw me coming and stopped to shake my hand. "Seeing the play made my stomach turn over with happiness," they said. "I'll never forget this night." I knew the words burst from their hearts, and that they spoke on behalf of everyone.

Later that night, after the generator ground to a halt, I lay in bed reflecting on how often I wanted to give up and forget putting on the pageant. Getting people from this culture to cooperate the way I expected them to was impossible. Now that the performance was over, however, and everyone who attended went home joyously and well versed in the true meaning of Christmas, I felt happy that I hung in there and didn't quit.

My thoughts took me back to those trying weeks of practices. Immediately, I knew *it was only the Lord* who kept me from giving up and calling off the pageant. Indeed, He was my ever-present help during those many nights of trouble.

Curling up in bed I reached for my pillow and hugged it — I was getting ready for what I knew would be the best sleep of the past two months.

"But You, O Lord, are a shield for me, my glory and the One who lifts up my head." Psalm 3:3 (NKJV)

"Enakaivo Natohwe A nuni vera ka'ene irama outihe namujina 'ee A nuni mavarasa'i maijina. A nuni nuana ahasirimihe veju'e sonahiuna." Samusi 3:3

Chapter 9

The Best Medicine for Healing

In 1962, when we first settled among the Managalasi people, the medical work we offered unlocked the door to our acceptance. Dispensing pills seemed a simple task, but to the minds of these people, it was as if we were dispensing miracles. Swallowing a few pills brought almost instant relief for their headaches, aching muscles or malaria; the antibiotic ointment we applied healed their sores and tropical ulcers quickly.

Being treated with our medicine worked like magic, and our efforts saved many lives. Saying "thank you" wasn't necessary — the words were written all over their faces, and gratitude shone from their eyes.

Now, just as in years long past, crowds roamed down from the village to our new home for medical treatment every afternoon at 5:00. The hour provided a social time as well, and folks who didn't need treatment joined the waiting patients on the verandah just for the camaraderie.

One day, out of the blue, we received a message from Mesise (messy-say), a young man who grew up with Rick and Randy. We were like family to him. Now, after taking medical training in the capital city of Port Moresby, he worked as a medic at the Sakarina Station which was in conjunction with the primary school.

Mesise's message read: *You should not be giving out medicine, you do not have any training. If the medical authorities find out what you are doing, you could get into a lot of trouble.*

His words felt like a shove from a bulldozer. I wondered what to do next when Poki, our first translation helper, now the village councilman, walked in the front door for a visit. Jim and I discussed the problem with him at length. Our discussion uncovered Mesise's true motivation: The medic complained because our free medical work drew people to us rather than to the mission station where payment was required.

Ever since our return to Numba, the decline in outpatients at Sakarina Station reflected poorly on the clinic's records. Since each patient had to pay a fee, the mission station was losing money, all because of our makeshift "clinic" in Numba Village. Jim and I weren't sure how to handle the problem.

"The walk to the station, the waiting time and then the treatment takes up most of the day," Poki revealed. "This means that on that day we can't work in our gardens."

"Maybe we should treat only the old people," Jim suggested. "The younger ones can easily walk to the station, but it's too stressful for the older people. They don't have the strength or energy to go up and down hills anymore."

"That's true," Poki agreed quickly, "but how about when we, the younger people, get malaria and don't have the strength to walk? We should be allowed to come to your house for medical help, too."

Jim thought about that a few minutes. "Allowing some younger ones, but not others will make it hard for the people to decide who has to go to the mission station and who doesn't."

"Yes, that would definitely be confusing," I agreed. "And you know we would probably help anybody who came for help, just to save them the two-mile walk. Then we'd wind up breaking our own rules."

When Poki left, we asked God what to do. After we prayed, we both felt confident that we should continue to help, not only older people, but everyone. The LVN licenses we held from our medical training in California gave us the competence to diagnose most cases, dispense tablets or apply ointment. If we were making the wrong decision to continue giving treatment, instead of feeling confident, we would have misgivings. We didn't.

Mesise tried to remain cordial to us whenever he came home to the village on his days off. Yet, his negative attitude caused an uncomfortable tension between us. It was difficult for him to look us in the eye when we talked, even after I explained about our medical credentials. Although the strain saddened me, I knew Jim and I had made the right decision.

The next morning we learned from the radio schedule that in a few days a plane would be going from Ukarumpa to Popondetta, then flying on to Port Moresby. Something within me leaped; I felt ready for a vacation, and this would be the perfect opportunity. I put my coffee cup down and looked at Jim. "Let's go to Moresby for a few days," I suggested. "It shouldn't cost too much to divert the plane from Popondetta to pick us up and then continue on to Port Moresby. What do you think?"

"Hmm, yeah," Jim agreed half-heartedly. "I suppose we could use a break from the village." His face brightened slightly. "I've been wanting to get my boots re-soled for a long time. This may be the chance I've been waiting for. I'll radio in and see if the flight coordinator could divert the plane to Sila Airstrip and shuttle us to Moresby."

In order to walk to Sila Airstrip, we had to pass through the grounds at the Mission Station. Knowing how the medical staff felt about us, I hoped we wouldn't meet any of them on our way. Fortunately, when we arrived at the station, no one was in sight. I breathed a sigh of relief. Jupo accompanied me, and we walked quickly across the mission property to the narrow path that wound down the mountainside to the airstrip. As I walked the last leg of the hike from the lower part of the airstrip to the top, I talked animatedly to Jupo. The hum of the plane's engine off in the distance announced its arrival. Right on time!

As the plane touched down, I looked at Jupo forlornly. She had become such a good friend, I hated to leave her behind. We stood staring at each other, and for a moment I thought we both would cry.

"I'll see you soon," I managed to say and removed my bag from her hand. She nodded in reply as I looked away quickly. Jim took the bag from me and placed it into the pod beneath the aircraft. Wasting no time, I climbed into the Cessna and fastened my seatbelt. As the plane lifted off the ground, I allowed myself to look back at Jupo. She watched the plane take off without expression and lifted her hand dismally in farewell. I waved back vigorously and settled back for the flight. Thirty minutes later, we landed on the airstrip in the capital city.

A blast of hot air seemed like it would barbecue me as we deplaned. Later, as we drove from the hangar to the Missionary Home, I noted the buildings built with genuine equipment, like timber, bricks and mortar, instead of jungle materials. Seeing normal traffic on the streets also lifted my spirits. As the Summer Institute of Linguistics (SIL) driver transported us to Mapang Missionary Home, we passed through the town of Boroko, just two blocks from our destination. As we rounded the corner, I caught a glimpse of the Brian Bell Building—my favorite place to shop. A few minutes later we pulled into the circular driveway of the Missionary Home. Still feeling excited, I got out of the vehicle and looked heavenward, taking time to thank the Lord for blessing us with accommodations requested at the last minute.

As Jim unloaded our suitcases from the van, the hostess greeted me cordially and handed me the key to our room. I walked quickly down the hall and unlocked the door. Once inside, I unnecessarily flipped the light on and off several times even though it was broad daylight outside. It seemed luxurious to see the lights go on without the use of a generator. And the hot water coming directly from the tap was another luxury I would never take for granted again.

Jim lugged our suitcases into the room and told me the good news: "No one signed up for the Land Cruiser! It's ours to use for the rest of the day!"

Hurriedly, I stuffed my bathing suit and beach towel into a handbag just in case there would be time for a swim at the hotel pool downtown. We put the remainder of our unpacking on hold and headed out the front door for town. Shopping, of course, was first priority. Both Jim and I brought long lists of things to buy for our Numba friends.

Jim parked the Land Cruiser in the post office parking lot where we thought it would be safe. Then we wandered up the street and into the hardware shop of the Brian Bell Building. Jim began looking for uninteresting things, like rake handles, bush knives and files to sharpen long machete-type knives. *Nothing exciting for me in here,* I thought.

"Jim, I'm taking the escalator to the shops upstairs. When you're ready to take your boots to be fixed, come and get me in the coffee shop!"

"Yeah," he said, as if my words hadn't penetrated his consciousness. I was out the door and moving up on the escalator when Jim caught my eye and waved. *He did hear.*

I eyed a few dresses and a pair of shoes, but nothing appropriate for village living, so I made my way to the end of the building where the coffee shop was located. The smell of fresh donuts drew me in. I felt ready for coffee.

"I'll have a cup of decaf and a donut," I told the cashier and handed her the exact coins. Looking around the shop, I spied an empty table in the corner. I sat down at the small square table and waited for the saleslady to bring my coffee and donut. It wasn't long before Jim walked into the coffee shop with Rexford, one of our Managalasi friends. Rexford worked in the Customs Department of the Immigrations Office. Jim and I felt proud of him for holding a government job. And, to our delight, he was free to join us for the rest of the day.

After I warmly welcomed Rexford, the three of us enjoyed donuts and drinks together. Then, we quickly descended the escalator and headed for the Land Cruiser to get Jim's boots. Jim fumbled with the keys to open the door for me. Just as I started to get into the vehicle, I got the surprise of my life! There, exposed on the front seat, lay my bathing suit. The beach towel had been tossed on the floor, and my unzipped handbag lay upside-down beside it.

"Someone broke into our vehicle," Jim said slowly, like he didn't quite believe what he was seeing. Quickly, I reached for my handbag and began putting the small articles that had been dumped on the floor back into the bag. Nothing seemed missing. Jim looked on the floor behind the driver's seat. "My boots are gone!" he announced.

Jim was upset for the rest of the afternoon. Those boots fit him very comfortably and, of all his footwear, those were his favorites. As for me, I was irritated that my swimming suit and towel with "California" printed in calligraphic lettering weren't good enough for the thieves; Jim's crummy old boots were the only things they took. Rexford, trying to console Jim, had a lot of unkind things to say about the thief.

By dinner time, Jim's anger had cooled down, and we returned to the coffee shop for a bite to eat. By this time several other Managalasi friends who worked in Port Moresby had joined us. They discussed the theft like it was headline news. "Sorry," they said to us repeatedly, shaking their heads and clicking their tongues in disapproval.

Inside the shop we slid two tables together, and the six of us sat down. Jim ordered hamburgers and Cokes for all of us, a treat our friends seldom, if ever, got to enjoy. When the hamburgers arrived, Jim motioned for me to give thanks.

"Lord," I began, "thank You that nothing valuable was stolen …," then, realizing what I had just said, I started to giggle. It was like saying that Jim's irreplaceable, prized boots were worthless. After a couple of snorts, laughter started tumbling out. Soon, it grew out of control, and I couldn't stop. But Jim wasn't laughing. He sat slowly shaking his head with a fierce look in his eyes that warned me to stop. But his reproof only made things worse, and the more I tried to stop, the harder I laughed.

I knew I was creating a bad scene because our Managalasi friends didn't understand why I was laughing. Finally, Jim gave up and finished the prayer for me.

After Jim finished, Rexford commented cautiously, "Jaki likes to play." He eyed Jim, then looked at me. Lastly, he lowered his eyes and took a big bite out of his burger.

Finally, back in control of myself, I casually mentioned to Jim, "If only the thief had turned your boots over and looked at the soles, he would have left the beat-up things in the car, taken off his own shoes and donated them to *you*." Jim remained straight-faced. Our friends at the table looked at me with a question in their eyes, and I knew they didn't understand my humor.

After the meal we promised to meet again the next day to shop for the things requested by our village friends. Then Jim and I drove off to the Mission Home to unpack.

The time passed all too quickly and within a few days we were on the Cessna flying back to the village. We landed in the early afternoon and, after bidding our pilot farewell, greeted the many friends who waited for us. After deciding who would have "the privilege" of carrying our suitcases and cargo, we began our hike home. As we passed through the Mission Station, Mesise's cousin rushed to meet us with a concerned look. "Mesise is sick and dying," he informed us. "He's in the hospital, would you go and see him?"

Feeling alarm, we moved quickly to the men's dormitory in the hospital. I recognized Mesise's relatives sitting around on the grass outside his room. Their grave expressions warned of impending mourning. Knots formed in my stomach as we passed solemnly by the family, nodding our heads to the few who looked up. When we arrived inside Mesise's room, he raised his head slightly.

"Ese," he greeted weakly, and explained what his symptoms were. "None of the medicine in the outpost has helped," he said finally. "Do you have anything?"

"I'm pretty sure we could find something to help," Jim replied. "We'll send you some medicine as soon as we can," he promised, and we left with Mesise's cousin trailing behind,

We hurried over the two-mile stretch from the hospital to Numba. We prayed diligently for God's wisdom in choosing the right medication to help Mesise recover. "It seems like he's got an infection of some sort," Jim suspected. "We'll try him on a dose of Amoxicillin and see if that helps."

As soon as we got home, Jim headed straight for the pantry and dug out the Amoxicillin from the medicine box. After scribbling a note with instructions for the dying man, Jim handed both medicine and note to Mesise's cousin, who stood on the porch waiting. The next day we heard that Mesise was sitting up, eating normally, and getting better. Relatives returning from the Mission Station stopped by to tell us that if it weren't for our medicine, Mesise would have died.

From that day onward, no one from the Mission complained about our dispensing medicine. To our minds, Mesise's recovery was an added confirmation from God that we had made the right decision to continue dispensing medicine from our home. In my heart I knew that the strain between our friend and us would now disappear.

"Thank you, Lord," I breathed. "Thank You for not only healing Mesise, but for restoring our relationship to what it should be."

"A new heart will I give you and a new spirit will I put within you, and I will take away the stony heart out of your flesh and give you a heart of flesh. And I will put my Spirit within you and cause you to walk in My statutes, and you shall heed My ordinances and do them." Ezekiel 36:26–27 (NKJV)

"Nara oja maiu'ina ja mihuna 'ee 'avena maiu'ina joni oja vaji ranahuna 'ee joni oja ka'ene muna sa'inijaho apene ruva'ikaivo oja ka'ene ajuasi'iniji mihuna. Enareje Nuni 'avena iji joni oja vaji ranahuna 'ee ijara ni'aji'eje ja Nuni irijara warama ja'ina'e 'urahohuna. Ene Nuni varapijaho hena veji'ina'e rehuna." Isikieri 36:26–27

Chapter 10

Unexpected News

The banana trees outside our window filtered a river of sunshine into the bedroom. I got up and dressed quickly. As I walked down the hall to the kitchen, an old tune came to mind, and I began to hum "Everything's Going My Way." I banged bowls and cups noisily on the table for breakfast as I sang the song, keeping one ear tuned for the sound of the plane's engine. Soon the aircraft would fly overhead to drop our mailbag somewhere close to the house before continuing on to Port Moresby.

"I'll try to drop it right at your front door," the pilot joked over the two-way radio last evening. He had spent the night with John and June Austing, who worked with the Omie people, about a seven-minute flight from our village.

I took the milk from the fridge and sat down at the table as Jim tilted a box of Cheerios into his bowl. Then, there it was—the low hum of the plane's engine in the distance.

"We better go," Jim said, setting the box of dry cereal down. "It'll only be a matter of seconds before the plane will be flying over the top of the village."

We pushed back from the table and rushed out. As we hurried across the church yard toward the village, the Cessna buzzed overhead, then rose high over the mountains and out of sight. We missed it!

"Now what?" I asked Jim.

"Let's see if anyone in the village saw where the mailbag landed."

"Okay," I agreed, "but I don't see many people wandering around yet. Could they possibly still be sleeping?"

At that moment, we heard a familiar voice:

"Jimmy-o! Jaki-o!"

We whirled around. It was Joshua's youngest brother Jon Mari running up the hill with the red mailbag. He knew how over-eager I behaved about the mail, so when he reached us, he thrust the mailbag straight into my arms.

Jon Mari, close friend and ready helper, tells us our mailbag dropped on his sister's roof.

"Where did it fall?" I asked, stifling my excitement.

"It landed on my sister Mainare's roof," he told us with a broad smile. "She didn't know the mail was coming today, and she screamed when she heard the thud. She thought her house was going to fall down."

Jim and I laughed as we imagined Mainare's shock. Then

the three of us walked back to the house together. I left the men talking in the kitchen and headed straight to the bedroom. There I turned the mailbag upside-down and dumped its contents on the bed. I fingered through the letters, searching for the familiar handwriting of family or friends. Then I spotted the letter I'd been waiting for.

It was Tanya's handwriting on a Seed Company envelope. By this time she had been working a few years as their graphic designer.

I tore open the envelope and pulled out the letter. "Dear Mom and Dad," it began, "You'll never guess how God answered my prayer to supply the money for Ted and me to fly out there and see you in New Guinea." I felt a spike of adrenaline.

"It happened on Bernie May's birthday," she continued. "I thought the "surprise" party was for him and I was helping Marguerite, his secretary, decorate the board room and arrange food on the table. I made a huge poster, and just as I was tacking it up on the wall some people started to arrive.

"'Hi, Tanya!' they said. I turned and was amazed to see that they were all *my* friends. *What in the world are they doing here at Bernie's party?* I wondered.

"Behind them came Bernie with Marguerite and my other office colleagues, Roger Garland, and Bill and Sharon Wells. 'Surprise, Tanya!' they yelled out and stared at me with expectant expressions, like they were waiting for me to do or say something. But I didn't understand what was going on.

"'What? It's not *my* birthday!' I told them. Then Bernie approached me with a twinkle in his eye."

"'It's my pleasure to present you with this gift from all of us in The Seed Company, plus a few other friends,' he said, stunning me. The smile never left his face, as if he wanted to laugh in surrender and say, 'We're glad we don't have to lie to you anymore about today's party.'"

"I reached for the envelope and looked at Bernie in disbelief. 'But, why?' I asked, not sure how to act. My hands started to shake as I opened the envelope. Then I pulled out *two round-trip tickets for Papua New Guinea!*

"I was overwhelmed. I had no idea they were planning this for Ted and me. I felt so unworthy. When I tried to thank them, no words would come; I just sat there with tears streaming down my cheeks. Then, one at a time, they came and hugged me, assuring me they would be praying for our safe trip."

Tanya was right — I never would have guessed that God would provide the funds for their flight to New Guinea through these friends. Delirious with the news, I ran down the hall crying and screaming at the same time, "Jim! Ted and Tanya are coming! The kids are coming!"

Jim sat at the kitchen table with Jon Mari drinking iced tea when I burst into the room. They jerked their heads toward me. Jim hadn't finished what he was saying, and his mouth was still open.

"Is it true?" Jon Mari asked immediately, "Are Tanya and her husband coming here? To Numba?"

"Yes!" I answered, and whirled around like a ballerina before his astonished eyes. "They arrive in Port Moresby on December 14th at 6:30 in the morning." Crazy with happiness, I squatted down to the floor and, arching my back while jumping up, I performed the cheerleader jump from my high school days. I could not contain myself, nor did I want to. Jon Mari smiled widely at me, as if genuinely amused.

"They'll spend Christmas with us here in the village!" I announced, and handed the letter to Jim.

As Jim began reading, I looked heavenward and breathed a prayer of thanksgiving: *Thank you, Lord Jesus, for giving me the desire of my heart. All praise be to You, Lord. Please bless everybody who gave money to make the trip possible for Ted and Tanya.*

"Though you have not seen him, you love him; and even though you do not see him now, you believe in him and are filled with an inexpressible and glorious joy." 1Peter 1:8 (NIV)

"Ja Hu pakavu vo ja Hu oja mahu 'ee ja Hu iviama pakavu vo ja Hu nimaa roju. Ijihuna'e ja ni'ima'ura temarasahe 'ee temaraka niho'o ira areri pa'warahunijino aromahuna." 1 Pita 1:8

Chapter 11

Tanya Arrives Home

The morning of December 14th dawned hot and thick in the capital city of Port Moresby. Ted and Tanya would be arriving in a few hours. Too excited to sleep, I shot up in bed at the Mapang Missionary Home, knowing I was short of the recommended eight hours of sleep by about seven hours. Just thinking about their arrival made my heart skip a beat. Maybe a couple of beats.

Jim and I arrived at the airport an hour early. It was already hotter than Hades even though the sky was overcast. Two years had passed since we'd last seen our daughter. Thoughts of being with her again kept the adrenalin rushing through my body. I stood against the chain-link fence staring hard at every plane that touched down. I wasn't aware if time was standing still or accelerating.

Finally, ten minutes earlier than scheduled, their jet arrived. After the aircraft pulled onto the tarmac and came to a halt, a stairway was wheeled to the front door for the passengers to exit. When it opened, my heart pounded like it would burst. I leaned into the fence as far as possible searching for Ted and Tanya's familiar frames among the many passengers. Suddenly, there they were! I spotted them the second they came out the door and began descending the short flight of steps. Both of them looked overwhelmed as

87

they walked in our direction, searching for us in the crowd of unfamiliar faces.

"Tanya! Ted!" I yelled above the turmoil.

They heard my voice over the airport noise, looked over and caught sight of us waving frantically. I heard a click and knew Jim's video camera was rolling. He video-taped them as they followed behind other passengers into the customs building. Ted looked uncomfortable in the wretched heat and drought-like conditions.

"Your luggage has to be inspected," I explained to Tanya who was looking back at us with anticipation.

"Okay, see ya later!" she replied, moving forward, but keeping her eyes on Jim and me.

The airport lounge in Port Moresby.

After we waited another nerve-wracking 30 minutes, the door of the customs building pushed open and out came our kids wearing the biggest smiles ever. Arms out, I ran over to my daughter and hugged her in a desperate embrace. I'd never been happier in my whole life. Jim's hand pressed my shoulder—he wanted his turn, too. Ted was next to be engulfed by my longing arms, and then we were ready to leave the airport.

"I didn't know it was going to be so hot here," Ted remarked, wiping his brow as we walked to the car.

"Hot and sticky, that's Port Moresby for you," I replied happily, not caring about the weather, as long as we were together. "You'll be much more comfortable in the village," I promised him.

"Where are we going now?" Tanya asked from the back seat.

"We'll go to the Mapang Missionary Home and get rid of the luggage," Jim said. "You can take a shower there if you want to, and then we'll go get something to eat."

"That sounds great! Can we go to the Coffee Shop?" Tanya asked.

"You bet!" I added and looked back to give her a knowing smile. "I'm not at all surprised that after being in America for 16 years, you still remember the Coffee Shop in Port Moresby."

"How could I forget our favorite place to hang out during vacations?" she replied.

Pulling away from the airport, Jim slowly navigated the roundabout at a traffic circle and took a local road to the Missionary Home. As we neared our destination, Tanya pointed out the sights she remembered.

As a family in years past, we would fly to the capitol city for vacations. While there, we visited the Brian Bell Building without fail and enjoyed shopping in the quaint shops. For Rick, Randy and Tanya, it was enough excitement just to ride the escalator up and down. Inevitably we stopped in the Coffee Shop for hamburgers at lunch time. We spent many happy moments in this little run-down shop, making good memories. Now, as we sat sipping our drinks, Tanya revealed a few of her misgivings.

"What if I get to the village and everybody expects me to speak the language?" she asked, looking worried. "I can understand most of what they say, but I can't speak much anymore. What should I do if they ask me a question?

"And another thing, what if I don't recognize my friends after all these years, especially my best friend Hilda?"

"Well," I said searching my mind for something positive to offer. "Ask God to help you," I said finally. "Our God is on standby, you know—an ever-present help. He promises to be there for us when we need Him."

On our day of departure for the village, the JAARS bus picked us up at Mapang Home and delivered us to the airport at 10:30 a.m. The Cessna had already arrived from Ukarumpa and was waiting for us on the tarmac. Tanya and I stood to one side while Jim and Ted transferred our luggage from the bus to the large scale where it would be weighed. I made certain they loaded the food I bought in town: fresh meat, cheese, Milo (a version of hot cocoa), Cornflakes, eggs and other items that were not available in the village.

After we weighed in on the scales, we boarded the plane. Jim sat next to the pilot, Alan Van Doren, and the three of us sat in the middle seat behind them. Minutes after take-off we were flying over green mountains of various shades and winding rivers. I glanced at Tanya. Her face was glowing as she stared down at the familiar scenery. Abruptly, she turned to look at me. "Mom," she said, her eyes shining, "I've come *home* at last!"

I was expecting the landing to be bumpy as usual, but Alan's landing was so smooth it felt like we had landed in butter. As we hurtled up the airstrip, I gaped out the window to see hundreds of people waiting along the side and at the end of the airstrip.

I saw Tanya take a deep breath.

Warriors with painted red faces rushed toward us as we deplaned. Dressed in g-strings made of bark, and feathered head dresses, they poised with spears held high as though to attack us. Ted wasn't sure what to do. With a wary look, he stood stock still, as if his feet had been nailed down.

The warriors noted his confusion and broke into smiles, stretching out their hands. "Ese!" they said, over and over, welcoming the new arrivals.

Tanya immediately responded with "ese" back to the greeters, not knowing for sure who to address. Ted followed suit. Hilda stood off to the left, crying. Tanya recognized her at once and ran to embrace her. Weeping, they locked in a long hug. Her friend, Aperohi, was next, then Lisa, all married women now, but their faces hadn't changed much; Tanya remembered them easily. The children of the three ladies stood staring, their eyes as big as Frisbees. Many other women stood by, whispering in audible admiration. I watched them all as they tightened their arms around Tanya as if she were a lost treasure now found and returned.

Jim and I organized the luggage and cargo to be carried while crowds continued to surge around Tanya and meet her husband. I looked around to see how Ted was holding up. I noticed the warmth of his smile as he looked beyond their scant clothing and strange faces painted red in war-like fashion. God helped him see the people underneath.

Many of the men spoke in English for Ted's sake, and he

was grateful. Jim's camera started to roll once again, recording this joy-filled reunion. For two years I had dreamed of this day, and it was exhilarating.

Soon we started our trek to the village. Ted stared in awe as the people shouldered boxes of cargo as though they were weightless and carried them up the steep trails to the Sakarina Primary School and Medical Station. As we followed along, Hilda took pineapple from her string bag. She had already cut it into bite-sized pieces.

"This is the sweetest pineapple I've ever tasted," Ted remarked as he savored piece after piece. How thankful we all were for Hilda who thought to bring the delicious, thirst-quenching fruit.

An hour later, we hiked past the small cemetery at the bottom of the hill that led into Numba Village. We were almost home. I glanced towards the top of the hill and saw a barricade made of palm branches and banana leaves blocking the entrance into Numba.

"Lisa!" I called out. "What's that fence doing there?"

"I don't know," she stammered, her eyes not meeting mine. The innocent look gave her away.

"Wait and see," Aperohi offered. "You'll find out soon."

Not much further to go. Turning around, I saw the warriors coming behind with grins on their faces. Then I heard Jim interrogating Poki, who walked beside him. Poki hemmed and hawed, not revealing anything.

Soon we stood outside the barrier, unable to go further. "Tanya!" Poki called out to her. "Knock on the gate!"

Tanya began to knock on the palm branch door.

A low voice on the other side asked her a question in Managalasi: "Who are you?"

Tanya replied in Managalasi: "I'm Jim Parlier's daughter."

"Why did you come?"

"I came with my husband to show him my home."

Upon hearing those words, the gate opened. Dancers dressed in bark cloth, with feathers in their hair, ushered us inside as they beat their drums. Hundreds more people welcomed Tanya to the village, her home for the first 11 years of her life.

They danced Ted and Tanya to the middle of the village where they had set up chairs around a large table of food. Yams, the main staple, were featured, and someone offered Ted one as soon as he sat down.

After saying thank you, he held it up for me to see. "Mom, is this okay to eat?"

"Yes, it's perfectly safe," I told him, and watched him bite off a piece of the potato. He mushed it around in his mouth for a while; I could tell he was struggling to swallow it. He looked up and saw me smiling at him.

"It's too bland, I need salt!" he commented, but to no avail. No one had thought to bring salt.

Aperohi's mother Sinaja wrapped a bark cloth around Tanya. Sinaja was as tiny as a child, with slender, birdlike fingers. "See if this fits," she said to Tanya, and, standing in front of her, bent down to wrap the bark cloth around her. Next, she secured the cloth with a woven belt made from the stems of plants. Finally, Hilda placed a brown woven headband on her head. Now she was all set to take part in the traditional dance.

"Come on, let's go," Hilda said, pulling her by the arm. "You're my partner, I'll show you what to do, just watch me."

Drums thundered as they joined the other dancers. The many spectators cheered loudly as Tanya joined in. They yelled to the people who stood around idly: "Come over here! Hurry! See Tanya dancing!"

The heavy drum beat fueled the hardy singing as frenzied

dancers whipped up high emotion. Jim and I walked to the sidelines to watch. Tanya moved her head up and down to the rhythm of the drum, imitating the other dancers. The singing and dancing got better and better by the minute. I couldn't stop smiling.

The following Sunday at church, Pastor Michael accompanied the hymns on his guitar. After the second song, Pastor Ivan asked Tanya to come up to the pulpit and speak. All heads in the church swiveled to watch Tanya stand and walk to the front.

Pastor Ivan calls Tanya to come up to the pulpit and speak.

"Don't be afraid," Pastor Ivan soothed when she reached the pulpit. "You can speak in English and I'll interpret for you."

Tanya smiled back gratefully, then began speaking to the family who had adopted her as their own. "I'm so glad that long ago God brought Mom and Dad here so you can know the truth and have eternal life," she began. I maintained a poker face, though I was thrilled to the core to hear her say these words.

"I loved growing up here and I hold on to every memory. Even though I no longer run with you barefoot down the path to the river, I gave you my heart as a little girl. No matter where I am, you are always a part of me."

I noticed Pastor Ivan choke up; he was having a hard time getting through all that Tanya was saying. She then ended quickly with the story of how God supplied the tickets so she and Ted could come. At this, Pastor Ivan broke down and cried. I looked around the congregation and saw almost everyone in the congregation crying with him.

"We prayed for many years that you would come back," Ivan said, wiping his eyes unashamedly. "Thank you for sharing with us how God answered our prayers."

As Christmas Eve approached, the believers planned to act out a play entitled "The Promise" taken from Isaiah 53. Pastor Michael would portray Isaiah. The Managalasis enjoyed play acting and loved to perform. Before they had a written language, the older people passed down historical information by acting out the events. This instilled in their minds the details that were somehow lost in the oral telling of it.

Another event in the Christmas program was the

performance of the Electric Slide to the tune of *Deck the Halls*. Tanya introduced the Slide number and practiced with the young women every day. Since their traditional dances were line dances, they picked up the footwork easily.

Of course, I had to join the women and girls for this event. Anything that bordered "wild" or "outlandish" drew me in. Together we buzzed around the church inside and out, practicing hard and often doubling over with laughter before we finally perfected the performance.

In-between the practice and laughter, Tanya and I kept busy baking cookies. In all, we baked over 800 to serve at the conclusion of the Christmas Eve service. Ted built a counter on the porch where we could easily serve everyone.

Decorating the Christmas tree was like bringing the lights of New York City to Numba. The tree stood tall in the corner of the living room in front of floor to ceiling louver windows. As soon as the sound of the generator started up, the entire village converged outside our house to watch the colored tree lights go on. Word spread, and soon people from other villages trekked to Numba to get a glimpse. They never failed to "Oooo" and "Ahhhh" as the tree lit up. Little children jumped up and down with joy. By the time December 24th rolled around, everyone was in the Christmas mood and ready for the service.

The program brought immense joy to the hearts of all who attended the performance. The evening didn't end there — everyone was invited to our house afterwards to hear about the meaning of the Christmas tree. Hundreds sat outside on the grass gazing at the tree through the window as we ushered groups of ten inside, offering them mats to sit on directly in front of the tree.

"The star at the top represents the star that led the wise men to the manger," I began. "The *red* decorations represent the blood Jesus shed on the cross to wash away our sins."

The group sat quietly, nodding their heads in agreement as they took in every word. "We understand now," they told me over and over. I felt a sense of accomplishment. Encouraged, I explained further: "The *green* of the tree means we have new life in Christ, and now we walk on the new road, which is God's way, not on the old road, which is our own way."

I saw their eyes fall to the gifts below. "We put gifts under the tree because God gave us a gift — *the very best gift.* He gave us His Son Jesus on Christmas day because He loves us. And so we give gifts to people we love on Christmas day, too."

With that I ended my short talk and accompanied each group in turn to the newly built counter for the Christmas cookies. Many thanked us over and over for the explanation and the cookies.

Marija, my village father, grasped my hand and held on to it. "Thank you for telling us the meaning of the Christmas tree," he said to me on his way out. "We always thought that worldly people who didn't believe in God put those trees in their houses at Christmas time. Now we know the truth."

The day after Christmas was Tanya's birthday. "There's no other place in the world I'd rather be on my birthday than down at the river," she announced over breakfast. Soon all her friends in the village knew of her request. Hilda came first, knocking on the door. Her husband followed with fishing gear. Several others tagged along.

"Come on, Tanya! Ted! Let's go down to the river!" they urged.

Standing at the kitchen window, I watched the group of about 12 scamper away and head down the path that led to the river. Since we would be leaving the village soon, I began to pack while they were gone. After six hours, Ted and Tanya returned, soaked to the skin, but grinning as they walked in the house.

"While we were swimming, the guys caught fish," Ted told us. "I was amazed at how many they caught in so little time. Then they wrapped the sardine-like fish in leaves and roasted them over the fire."

"The water was freezing, and it took Ted forever to get in," Tanya added, then looked at Ted and laughed. "Later, when they brought the fish over for us to eat, Ted took a long time hesitating over that, too."

"Yeah, they expected me to eat the whole thing—head and all!" Ted exclaimed, looking uneasy. "'Put it all in your mouth,' they told me. So I forced the whole fish down in one bite. I was surprised I couldn't tell any difference in texture or taste between the head and the body."

"You did it, Babe, and I'm proud of you," Tanya confirmed, still smiling as she patted him on the shoulder. Then, turning to me, she said: "But now we're really hungry, Mom. What's there to eat?"

Time flew by too quickly, and departure day arrived. Tanya didn't feel ready to leave yet, but knew that it had to be. I could tell she grieved as she went around the village to say goodbye. "Ese," she said to each person, shaking their hand.

"Godi merajaho!" (God bless you) came the tearful replies. People throughout the village heard Hilda's wailing. Overcome with sorrow, Tanya could barely respond to her friends' goodbyes. When she reached Pastor Ivan's house she asked, "Is this the last time I will see my Managalasi family? My village home? The mountains and the river?"

Pastor Ivan thought for a few minutes before replying: "We, as human beings, think there won't ever be a way for us to be together again, but God is in control. He wants you to trust Him for everything, and if He wants you to come back, He will make the way possible."

"Commit your way to the Lord, trust also in Him, and He shall bring it to pass." Psalm 37:5 (NKJV)

"Oni 'unamijija Natohwi jihuni ija tahi irechame Hu nimaa vetiakame Hura vena'amana." Samusi 37:5

Chapter 12

A Question of Commitment

Coffee-picking season arrived—the season when all other activities ceased. Without exception, everyone put normal garden work, literacy classes and building projects on hold. All focus would now be directed entirely on picking the cherry-colored berries, removing the hulls and drying the beans in the sun. This important work took top priority so that when the coffee was sold, families would be able to pay for their children's school fees. Without payment, a child could not have the privilege of attending grade school at Sakarina Primary School or the high school in Popondetta.

In spite of the busyness of coffee work, wives put pressure on their husbands to help with other chores or with taking care of the children. Jim knew it would be impossible to get any revision work done by staying in the village during coffee season, so he booked a flight to Ukarumpa. At Wycliffe's Center he and his translation helpers would be able to work in uninterrupted bliss. To our relief, Joshua and Aparihi agreed to come with us.

Joshua, the son of my village father Marija, a village chief, had inherited his father's wisdom for showing discernment and making superior choices relating to problems. We relied on Joshua, knowing that with his input, the New Testament revision would be excellent. He had quit his job teaching third graders at the Sakarina Primary School. To our delight, he was now devoted full time to translation.

Joshua Sovi helped make the New Testament revision an excellent one.

Aparihi was also diligent and thorough in his work. He never replied haphazardly, but thought things through before speaking his opinion. Jim and I agreed we had two of the best men in the village helping us do translation work. And so, with high hopes, we prepared to leave the village and continue work at Ukarumpa.

Jupo, Joshua's daughter, had also inherited her grandfather's intelligence. Rarely did I have to explain anything twice. As we checked the corrections the men were making, I relied heavily on her suggestions. Then we submitted our changes for the committee to consider.

"Yes, it's true," the checkers would agree, "Jupo's way of wording this sentence makes it clearer."

The young woman was becoming more and more valuable

to me, and I never made a decision in regard to the translation without asking her opinion first.

Departure day to Ukarumpa arrived. Isoro knocked on
the door at sunup to suspend our mattress to the rafters
where the rats couldn't get to it while we were gone. I looked
in the pantry for something quick to make for breakfast.
Grabbing the oatmeal off the shelf, I lit the stove and boiled
the water as Jim and Isoro carried the generator from the
shed to Jim's study for storage. Jupo secured boxes of matches
and food items in sealable containers. Isoro's closest friend
Taiva cleaned out the kerosene refrigerator and gave away
the leftovers to some of the ladies who sat patiently on the
porch waiting to say goodbye.

As usual, it was difficult to leave the village. Our extended
family depended on our help for so many things. Especially
medicine.

"It's because you weren't here, that's why Sumeta died,"
they accused the last time we were away doing work at
Ukarumpa. "Your medicine would have saved him!"

In many cases this was true. Lives were spared because of
the antibiotics we dispensed. Now, Niaka, Chululu's older
brother, lay out in the sun shivering beneath an old towel.
I fished out all the leftover flu medicine from our medicine
box, enough to last two days, and handed it to Sinaja, his
wife. "Tell Niaka to eat two pills when the sun comes up,"
I instructed, "then two more when the sun is straight overhead, and two more when the moon comes up."

Sinaja looked at me with sad eyes, as though her husband had died already. She nodded when I grasped her hand and held on to it tightly.

Jupo picked up the cat and gave him one last hug before putting him into his cage. The Cessna would be landing in about an hour, the amount of time it took me to walk to the airstrip. Jupo grabbed my suitcase as we hurried out of the house and up through the village, stopping briefly to say goodbye to friends. A bunch of kids tagged behind PK, our Shih Tzu dog, and took turns carrying the cat.

In my heart, I wished Jupo were coming with us, but Kirija, my former kitchen helper, was already living in Ukarumpa. Even though he was presently employed by the Guest House manager, I knew he would come on Saturdays and some evenings to help me. When it came to cooking and cleaning, Kirija had plenty of experience and did a thorough job.

His main job at Ukarumpa was to take care of the dorm quarters for the translation helpers who accompanied their teams to the Center to do language work. Kirija also mowed lawns, kept the dorms clean and supplied whatever was necessary to keep the men happy while they were away from their villages.

Just as I reached the airstrip the Cessna flew in and landed. While Jim and the pilot loaded the plane, I said a hurried goodbye to everyone who had come to see us off, with special goodbyes to Cracker and Pupudi who would be missing the help of their husbands during this busy season. The pilot did a quick turn-around, and we landed in Ukarumpa an hour and a half later—just before the grocery store closed. What a treat to be able to shop in the Base store again. I rushed through each aisle buying groceries for the two men as well. New cake mixes and candy bars from both America and Australia stocked the shelves. What a sight for tired, chocolate-starved eyes! I planned to provide evening meals for the men so that they would only have to prepare breakfast and lunch for themselves.

The day after our arrival we began the tedious process of revising the New Testament. As we expected, Joshua and Aparihi worked well together, producing top-quality revisions. Their work would later be checked again by a competent committee in Numba to ensure that the vocabulary and grammar used were natural and appropriate. My job was to enter the corrections for each book after the men made the changes.

Each day brought about a measure of achievement and satisfaction for the four of us.

Today I set a goal to type in corrections for the first ten chapters of 1 Corinthians. I had just started chapter 7 when the power for the entire Base shut down. My computer went dark, followed by a crack and a sizzle. Fortunately, I had been saving my work after every two verses, so I felt sure I hadn't lost any translation.

At that moment, the aroma of Kirija's banana cake baking in the oven reached my nostrils. *Warm cake would be great with a cup of coffee right about now,* I thought, and checked my watch. It was almost 11 a.m. Unexpectedly, the power suddenly came back on. Quickly, I checked my morning's work on the computer. Chapters 5 through 7 were gone!

My heart dropped. I would have to retype those chapters, and chapter 7 was so long.

Feeling aggravated, I headed for the kitchen to get that cup of coffee. Grabbing a teaspoon out of the drawer, I spooned in some decaf when the phone rang. It was the Radio Shack.

"Is Pastor Michael there?" the radio operator asked, referring to Aparihi.

"No," I replied, "but I can take a message to him right away."

"A man named Chululu called in on your radio this morning to give him a message—Tell him that his Uncle Varisi is very sick."

"Who?"

"Varisi—Victor, Alpha, Romeo, India, Sierra, India," the operator repeated patiently.

"Thank you, I'll take the message to Pastor Michael right away," I said, and hung up.

I moaned inwardly. Knowing how close the relationship was between Varisi and Aparihi, I wondered how I would break the news to him. Another thought that slowed my steps to the cubicle was knowing how the information would definitely delay the revising progress.

I put several pieces of Kirija's banana cake on a plate and made my way down the road to the translation cubicle where Jim, Joshua and Aparihi were working. When I walked in with the treat, all three looked up expectantly.

"Jaki, ese!" they greeted happily, obviously unprepared for bad news.

"Kirija just baked this, and it's still hot," I announced without a trace of the forthcoming announcement. I flipped on the electric kettle to make coffee for the boys and tea for Jim. Then, catching Jim's attention, I motioned for him to join me outside.

Jim groaned when I told him what the radio operator reported. "Satan is trying his best to keep us from getting the revision finished," he replied, summing up the situation.

Helplessly, I agreed, knowing that if we had to send Aparihi back to the village, the revision would come to an abrupt halt. Jim would not feel assured using only one man to make all the decisions; he needed both to discuss problem areas, to make decisions together and thereby bring about an accurate translation, one he would feel confident in.

Feeling forlorn, I went back inside the cubicle. When I saw that Aparihi was fixing the coffee, I left and walked slowly back up the hill, leaving Jim to break the news. Retyping three chapters was trivial compared to what Jim would have to face with this setback.

Aparihi's reaction was expected. He asked Jim to book his return flight to the village immediately. Seeing that further checking for the day was useless, Jim left the cubicle, got into the car and drove the five miles to the hangar to book the distressed man's flight. Fortunately, a plane would be going to Port Moresby on Friday and could easily divert to Sila Airstrip and drop off Aparihi. This left two days for Jim to finish a bit more revision.

That night, I prepared supper for the men as usual, and used my new recipe for squash. It required apples, butter and brown sugar. *The men were going to like this dish,* I thought. Still, because of Varisi's illness, I anticipated a depressing evening. The thought prompted me to walk to Dorelo Home while dinner was baking to rent a video.

Dorelo Home was named after three Australian expatriates, Doris, Elsie and Olive Dorelo. These elderly sisters had given many years of their lives to be "aunties" to the children whose parents did translation work in their villages. The sisters cared for each child in their home as though they were their own, and the children loved them dearly. So did everyone at the Center.

The house was still used as a children's home with the

added feature of video cassettes that could be rented for a small fee. When I arrived, several teenagers stood browsing through the shelves of videos. They looked excited, giggling and chatting together. How grateful I felt to Jeff and Sue Russell for working out details and providing appropriate videos so the residents of Ukarumpa could enjoy relaxing at home with a movie in the evenings.

Almost immediately, I spotted a John Wayne movie. Knowing how much Jim and the two men enjoyed watching westerns, I happily signed out the video and rushed home to finish dinner.

Talk at the dinner table didn't come easily that night. Aparihi avoided eye contact with both Jim and me. Towards the end of the meal, Jim cleared his throat and looked at both men. "Did God really call you to do translation work, or to just translate when it's convenient?"

Aparihi looked down at his plate, but Joshua eyed Jim directly: "God called me to do this work," he replied boldly, "otherwise I wouldn't be here now. I'd be back at Sakarina teaching 3rd graders."

Jim nodded his head and proceeded to explain, using our situation as an example. "God called Jaki and me to give you His Word in your language. That's the reason we never counted the cost of separation from family—or any inconveniences. This is where God wants us right now, and we trust Him to take care of the problems at home."

Aparihi looked thoughtful as he turned to face Jim. This seemed like my clue to disappear, so I quickly stood up and cleared away the dishes. As I carried them into the kitchen, a conversation began at the table. When Aparihi spoke, I noted that the tenseness in his voice was gone. Guardedly, I observed him from the kitchen and noted that he seemed more relaxed now than when he had arrived for supper.

I rinsed the dishes and banged pots around for a while, giving the men time for discussion. After 40 minutes, I felt we all had endured enough seriousness for one day and marched to the video tape player to insert the video. Then I turned to face the three figures at the table. "The movie is ready!" I announced exuberantly. All three stood promptly and joined me in the living room. I could tell they were mentally ready to switch gears. Listening to our translation helpers laugh the remainder of the evening was the best way to end a trying day.

The next morning as Jim and I were eating breakfast, Aparihi called. "My heart is healed," he told Jim. "You can cancel my flight home. I'll stay another two months and fly home with you, Jaki and Joshua."

Jim and I were amazed. We knew it was God who intervened and turned Aparihi's heart around. With thankful hearts, Jim and I prayed, giving God all the glory.

The following Sunday morning Aparihi's wife Virginia scheduled a 9:00 a.m. conversation. We all wanted to know the village news, so the four of us walked down the hill together to the Radio Shack. To our surprise, Uncle Varisi was up and waiting to talk on the other end.

"I'm doing okay," he assured his nephew. "I wish you were here, but I know you're doing God's work."

Then Virginia took the receiver: "Four doctors from Norway are coming to our village and will live in the literacy house. They want to practice medicine here and are going to stay for two months."

That news brought relief to all of us. Having real doctors living in Numba meant that not only Varisi and Niaka would have good medical care, but everyone in the village would receive professional help. What a load off our minds! Feeling lighthearted, the four of us left the Radio Shack to attend the morning worship service in the meeting house.

The following weeks went smoothly. We worked long hours night and day to get the job done. When it was time to go to bed, every muscle in my shoulders ached. Hot showers helped. Water was not a problem at Ukarumpa and while there I never had to concern myself about the shower bucket emptying before I finished rinsing off the soap.

Jim and the men started to revise 1 Thessalonians. Once they accomplished this, only eleven New Testament books would be left to check. Still, all the corrections and changes would have to be checked by a committee in the village before the printing could take place. The road to a finished product seemed miles away, but each day I awoke with a sense of excitement and utter joy. God had given me the best, most satisfying life ever!

Aparihi continued to have radio conversations with his wife on Sunday mornings. Virginia never failed to mention the conditions at home that required her husband's attention, the biggest problem being the roof. "The leaves are worn and shredding, and the roof is leaking badly. We sleep close to the outside walls," his wife informed him, "but still, *your* children get up wet and cold in the mornings."

After that last conversation, Aparihi began acting differently again. Instead of focusing his attention on the New Testament changes, all he talked about was the work he should be doing in the village — how his house was in shambles and about to fall over. Or how the men he had asked to cut wood for his new house were sick and didn't have strength to carry the heavy wood from the jungle to his building site.

At one point both men were in a foul mood, upsetting Jim as well. They had hit a brick wall in the revision process and were not accomplishing much. Feeling disgusted over this turn of events, Jim left the men pouting at the table in the cubicle and headed for the Radio Shack. There he wrote a message for the radio operator to send out the following morning to Poki.

"Hire some guys to cut new pandanus leaves and fix Aparihi's roof," Jim instructed. "Tell them they'll get paid when we get back to the village at the end of June."

In the store I was delighted to find veal cutlets on sale. That night I dipped them in eggs and bread crumbs before frying, just like Mom taught me. Eating meat prepared in this fashion would be a first for Joshua and Aparihi. Next, I prepared a brown sugar, butter and marshmallow mixture to pour over the sweet potatoes before baking them. *The men will never forget this meal*, I thought. We would eat Kirija's butter cake for dessert in the living room while watching the video, *Free Willy 3*.

That evening, Joshua and Aparihi arrived looking forlorn. They took their places at the table without uttering a word. Turning up the music, I served dinner as cheerfully as possible. I handed Joshua the veal cutlets, and his eyes lit up. "What kind of meat is this?" he asked, observing the strange-looking food.

"What's this white stretchy stuff on the sweet potatoes?" Aparihi wanted to know. Before long, we were all eating our supper with gusto and in high spirits. What started out to be a bad day was ending well. I knew the prayers of our supporters had carried us through another faith-stretching day. What would we do without those prayers?

Thank you, Lord Jesus," I prayed silently. *"Thank You for every church, friend and supporter You have blessed us with, enabling us to do this work, especially on days like today.*

"I will bless the Lord at all times; His praise shall continually be in my mouth." Psalm 34:1 (NKJV)

"Na vekuveku Natohwijaho taarohuna. 'Ene Hu taarohujaho na'ia mapoka nuni ira vaji ro usevi nahuna." Samusi 34:1

Chapter 13

Going Back Home to Numba

On the morning of our flight back to the village, the aviation bus arrived at 6:30. The driver packed our luggage and cargo carefully into the back of the bus and drove the four of us to the hangar. Friends Bob and Ruth Merz waited there to bid us farewell. During our stay at the Center we had dined in their home several times. Since Aparihi and Joshua spoke English, the Merzes came to know them very well.

The chilly air caused steam to rise from their faces as they welcomed us off the bus. "We thought you decided not to go to the village today," Ruth laughed. Her smile warmed my heart. We stood chatting and laughing until our pilot Rick Nachtigal approached us. "It's time to go," he announced. I looked at my watch—7:30.

"Wow!" I said, amazed. "This is the earliest we've ever been able to take off." But the clouds had lifted, and the plane was ready for us to board. What a beautiful day to fly. The skies were already blue with hardly a cloud. I felt no sadness at leaving Ukarumpa. Numba Village was our true home, and the Managalasi family God had given us waited there for our arrival.

Friends, Bob and Ruth, come to see us off at the hangar.

As the plane lifted, we waved our goodbyes to Bob and Ruth who stood at the edge of the airstrip waving heartily. An hour and a half later we were waving to the jubilant figures below who jumped up and down in the middle of the village as we circled overhead. Thankfully, many friends and school children waited on Sila Airstrip to help carry the boxes of food supplies and other cargo which would see us through the next six weeks in the village.

Jupo's face was the first I saw, filling me with happiness as I climbed down from the plane. All stood to one side watching as Jim organized the cargo and designated carriers for each box. With that done, he went on ahead with the men as Jupo and I fell behind. Jupo guided PK on his leash, pulling gently whenever the dog stopped to check out the bushes along the trail. The walk to Numba wound uphill all the way, and PK's stopping to sniff at every blade of grass gave me a good excuse to slow down and rest whenever I needed to.

Once I reached the lower part of the village, a spunky Managalasi chorus spontaneously sprung from my mouth:

"All you people, get out of my way — this is my road! This is my place!"

Older women who sat in their doorways grinned from ear to ear. They nodded their heads in rhythm as I sang.

"Yes, Jaki, this is your place! You're home again!" they shouted back in welcome.

They loved hearing me sing in their language, not caring if I sang on key or not. I squeezed my eyes shut, unashamedly forcing out all the tears. *I was home.*

Later in the day, Jupo washed all the dishes and pots and then wiped out all the kitchen cupboards with antiseptic liquid as I unpacked. She worked diligently and thoroughly, doing everything exactly as I wanted. Jupo thought of herself as our daughter; I thought of her as my best friend, a special gift from God.

Isoro looked over each box of cargo as it arrived at our house. "You've got two umbrellas!" he declared in an accusing voice, pointing to the umbrellas. "One of those is mine!" he announced, and carried them into the bedroom where he hung them on the doorknob. Not many villagers owned umbrellas; most used large banana leaves to shield themselves from the rain. Isoro glowed with his special find. Since he was Jim's close friend, he didn't think it necessary to ask if he could have the umbrella, his status with Jim automatically made whatever he claimed his.

Next Isoro picked up the broom and, after sweeping the bedroom, untied the ropes that suspended our mattress from the rafters. "What else has to be done?" he called out to Jim. No doubt about it, Isoro was Jim's right-hand man.

That evening, when Jim tried to start the generator, the rip cord was tight and wouldn't turn. "No lights tonight," he told me. Without being asked, Kwaare brought over his kerosene lamp so we could see well enough to put sheets on the bed. Around eight o'clock Jim blew out the light, and we settled down under the covers ready for sleep.

Moments later I heard a noise in the hallway. Then I remembered we had forgotten to lock the door. I turned over and sat up. In the twilight, I saw a tall dark figure remove an umbrella from the doorknob and leave.

"Blessed is the man who perseveres under trial, because when he has stood the test, he will receive the crown of life that God has promised to those who love Him." James 1:12 (NIV)

"Ea ka'ene venakia hari majamano kirana va'amajaho Godira merajahuna. Ijihuna'e hu nimaa'e kirane va'ana'e re'amajaho hu majama hihuni i'esa ka'ene natohwijara ea ka'ene Hu oja mahuji nahama 'waramajaho apehuna." Jemisi 1:12

Isoro, the "umbrella thief," comes to the house often to help Jim.

Chapter 14

Translation Setbacks

After four weeks in the village, Jim began to feel discouraged with progress on the translation checking. A deadline for completion loomed over him, but both of our main translation helpers stayed busy with other projects and did not come to work. Aparihi was building his new house, so we didn't expect him to come, but where was Joshua? He hadn't shown up once since our return.

One day Jim met Joshua on the road and reminded him about the deadline. "We really need to work on revising the translation," he said. "When will you be able to come and help?"

"Oh, okay," Joshua replied. "I'll come a little later on today."

Jim waited and waited, but Joshua never showed up. Then Jim learned from others that Joshua had gone off to work in his garden. *Was our main translation helper making a statement of some kind through the empty promise he made to Jim?*

We had no clue as to why Joshua was not coming to check translation with Jim and the Committee. His actions were taking their toll on Jim. Noting Jim's anguish made me angry with Joshua. If the man had any integrity, he would just tell Jim he was quitting. Then perhaps Jim could get another helper and move on. The uncertainty was stressing us both out.

Stalling, I asked myself, *What is forgiveness, anyway?* The dictionary states it is "a deliberate act of releasing someone from an act of wrongdoing." In other words, it was up to *me—I* would have to make the effort. But I wasn't ready to forgive Joshua yet. So I went on pretending not to see him.

God answered the prayers we requested, but not as we expected. Joshua's older daughter Kumari arrived home for a vacation from the university in Port Moresby and asked to help check the corrections to the translation.

"Okay," I told her. "Jupo could probably use a break for a week or two." Her helping me required the reading of each New Testament book aloud from beginning to end. Kumari could read faster than anyone I knew, including me. How thankful I was that she could take time off from her job at the coffee shop in the Port Moresby Islander Hotel to be in the village this month. She quickly pointed out several sentences either with incorrect grammar or hard-to-understand concepts.

Spelling Bible names proved to be one of the biggest walls for us to penetrate. Since there were no b's, l's, x's or z's in the Managalasi language, names like Arphaxad and Beelzabub were impossible. But with Kumari's suggestions, we waded through, changing some of the letters so it would be easier for a Managalasi to read, yet be as close to the true pronunciation as possible.

At the end of each day, I handed Jim a page of corrections with suggested spellings to check with Chululu. Jim would sigh, and the weary look in his eyes seemed to ask: "Will our checking and re-checking with the committee never end?"

Working with Kumari, however, didn't seem laborious because of the laughs we shared. One afternoon, just before going home, she remarked: "Jaki, I'm reading too much Bible."

"What do you mean?" I asked, perplexed.

"When I go back to work at the coffee shop in Moresby, I won't be able to steal any more chocolate cake with a clear conscience."

Too many interruptions in the village prevented progress on the translation checking, the biggest setback being Joshua not coming to help. To resolve the problem, Jim decided to go to Ukarumpa and take the translation committee. Ukarumpa would be a wonderful get-away, and the committee would love to go with us.

Joshua's wife, Kwaka, whom I nicknamed Cracker, came faithfully every evening to help dispense medicine. She assured us over and over that her husband would return to Ukarumpa with us. *Would I be disappointed if Joshua didn't come?* I asked myself. Of course we needed his expert help, yet I felt relief at the thought of his staying behind. That would end the hurt and stress that came from his ignoring us.

The day before we flew out, Jim installed a solar system to light up the inside of the church. The villagers, thinking it would be impossible, had never asked Jim to install a light. They believed that only wealthy people, or those who lived in cities, could enjoy such luxury.

When Jim finished the installation, he told Aparihi he was ready to light up the church. By this time crowds of excited villagers gathered inside practically filling the building. It was hard to believe there would be lights in *their* church building — they had to see it to believe it.

Jim glanced at me as he reached for the light switch. "I hope it'll work," he said with a doubtful look. One flick of the switch proved his doubting to be in vain — the church lit up immediately. Every face glowed with awe. It took a few seconds for reality to sink in. Then deafening cheers erupted, drawing the entire village to the church site. No one wanted to miss out on this historic event.

Based on Cracker's words that Joshua would return to Ukarumpa with us, Jim booked him a seat on the plane. The

aircraft could accommodate seven passengers: four translation helpers, Jupo, Jim and me. The checkers, Poki and Isoro,
would have to go by ship.

While at Ukarumpa Jim planned to go over the final draft
from Matthew to Revelation and make any changes necessary.
This would be the most critical reading. After finishing this
task, we would take the final copy to the print shop and
submit it for typesetting. The manuscript would then be
sent to Korea to be printed.

Since the 402 could not land on our small airstrip, a helicopter flew in to shuttle us to Popondetta where we would
wait for the larger aircraft to take us to Ukarumpa. I felt
overjoyed that Jupo would be coming this time. She and
I were on the first shuttle along with most of the luggage.
When we reached Popondetta, we searched for a shady place
to wait. The airport offered little shelter from the sun, and the
air was stifling. Even the birds were too uninspired to chirp.

Fortunately, the helicopter pilot brought the mailbag, so
I settled down on the grass in the blistering heat to read
the mail. Jupo sat down and leaned back against an old tire
that lay against the SIL shed where she promptly fell asleep.
After a while, two men walked by staring at us as they passed.
Tongue in cheek, I asked, "Where can I buy an ice-cold Coke?"

"Oh, I've got some over here," one of the men replied,
shocking me. I had no inkling of an idea that Cokes would
be available on the Popondetta airstrip. The man pointed
to a small shed across the road. The building was weathered
and falling apart.

"Jupo! Come on!" I squealed, waking her.

"What?" she said sleepily, rubbing her eyes.

"These men said they know where we can buy Cokes!
Let's go!"

My curiosity piqued, I helped Jupo to her feet, and we

followed the men across the dirt road. I tried to keep my soaring hope for a cold Coke in check. *Fat chance there's going to be cold Cokes here,* I told myself so I wouldn't be too disappointed. The first man unlocked the door to a five by seven-foot room where an ice chest lay on the floor. He pulled open the lid revealing some cold Cokes and Oreo cookies. *Thank You, Lord, for sending along this man at just the perfect time.*

"They cost K1.20 (60 cents) each," he told me apologetically, not knowing that at that moment I would have paid K5 for one. Quickly, before I woke from this dream, I paid the man for two Cokes and one packet of Oreos. Sipping an ice-cold Coke and eating Oreo cookies while I read the mail made the two-hour wait on the hottest airstrip in the world more bearable.

Before I finished the last bit of mail, the drone of the helicopter in the distance made its soon-arrival apparent. Jupo and I watched as it half-circled the field and landed. Pastors Ivan, Michael and Chululu slowly stepped down from the aircraft. Then, a few seconds later, Joshua followed. "Your father really did come!" I remarked to Jupo.

"Yeah," she agreed, clearly unimpressed.

When the pilot saw Jupo and me, his eyes widened. "Where did you get those Cokes?" he asked, amazed. "Are they cold?"

Jim, upon hearing my reply, immediately headed across the dirt road to buy Cokes for the pilot and for each of the team.

Ahhh, a rare sight — happy faces on the Popondetta airstrip!

"Your love has given me great joy and encouragement, because you, brother, have refreshed the hearts of the saints."
Philemon 1:7 (NIV)

"Vwea nune ara ea oja mihujara reju'e na niho'o teamanime oja sonahie 'ee Godoni ehija mapoka ijara ni'ajihu." Pairimani 1:7

Chapter 15

Our Glorious Future Bodies

Standing in the sunlight in front of our house at Ukarumpa, all four members of the translation team shivered. The village elevation of 2,500, to which they were accustomed, was half of the 5,200-foot elevation on the Center, and the men struggled to adjust.

"Come on in the house and sit down," I offered, although inside our house wasn't much warmer than outside. Still, the cozy atmosphere of our living room was inviting. Not without exertion, Chululu, Aparihi, Ivan and Joshua labored up the five steps onto our small porch which led into the house.

"Jim will be here any minute," I assured them, mustering up as much cheer as I could. They flopped down wordlessly on the couch and armchairs to wait. Today Poki and Isoro would arrive to join us at Ukarumpa and help with the revision work. They boarded the ship in Oro Bay, just south of Popondetta, and sailed to Lae. From there they caught a Public Motor Vehicle (PMV) to Kainantu, a town about a 20-minute drive from Ukarumpa.

After a few minutes of small talk, Jim drove into the driveway with the Center's van. The sight of the vehicle sparked some life in the men, and their dismal expressions evaporated as we left the house and piled into the van for the trip to Kainantu.

We drove through a small village outside of Ukarumpa and wound uphill around a small mountain to a flat road that took us into town. It wasn't long before we pulled up to the corner truck stop where we had previously arranged to meet the two men.

Poki and Isoro had arrived early. They stood at the truck stop with their baggage, looking up and down the road incessantly as they waited. As soon as they caught sight of us, the weariness seemed to shrivel from their faces. We got out of the van quickly and both men pumped our hands vigorously, their faces glowing with happiness. Within seconds we were all laughing and talking at once.

Poki, a born storyteller, waited for just the right moment to tell us about their overnight voyage on the ship. Most of his stories contained the truth, but Poki loved to add an outlandish detail or two for dramatic effect. He couldn't help himself.

"The winds were so bad that I thought our ship would get tossed up into the sky," Poki began. "Babies wailed and people vomited everywhere—they couldn't make it to the railing. Nobody got any sleep. Then, when it was time to disembark, we couldn't walk—we felt too dizzy."

"I couldn't stay on my feet," Isoro chimed in, adding to the drama. He leaned to one side and hobbled so we'd get the picture. "I had to grab hold of the railing and hold tight, or I would have fallen down into the water and drowned."

We laughed heartily as Isoro relived his experience. Poki, his eyes still bright with mischief, told how they quickly found where to catch the PMV. "One just happened to be waiting when we got to the truck stop in Lae," he declared.

"We were hungry when we got on the truck," Isoro added,

"but now we're starving! Did you bring us any food to eat?"

We hadn't, so once again we piled into the van. Jim drove around the Kainantu airstrip and followed the road that wound around to the hotel. The red poinsettias that bloomed all year long stood out boldly against green hedges on both sides of the road. Joy swelled up inside as I thought about going to the hotel to eat — a rare privilege.

Inside the hotel, after we were seated, we easily reached a unanimous decision — everybody wanted hamburgers and fries. We held hands around the table as Aparihi gave thanks. Before he asked God's blessing on the food, he thanked the Lord for the safe arrival of the two men, then asked for help to accomplish the goal for which they had come, asking the Lord to enable them to work well together as a team while making the necessary changes. We all said a hearty "Amen" to that!

One morning as I mixed batter for raisin oatmeal cookies, my heart stirred restlessly. God told us to leave our burdens at His feet, so why was I carrying around this anger over the rift with Joshua? *Would I have to keep on confessing the sin of not forgiving him every day for the rest of my life?*

In Psalm 112, David said: "When darkness overtakes the righteous, light will come bursting in." *Well, life sure seems dark to me now, Lord. How will You work this out? Yet, I believe You will work it out, Lord, and until then, I'll keep looking for that light You promised to come bursting in.*

I recalled long-ago days when Joshua was like our son.

Our love and caring for each other was mutual. The boy would have done anything to help Jim or me. Back in the year 1981, as we prepared to go home to America, just months after Cracker gave birth to Jupo, they carried the infant to our doorstep. With the baby cradled in his arms, Joshua announced, "You're leaving us, and we wanted to give you a gift. We have nothing valuable to offer, so Cracker and I agreed to give you our baby daughter, Jupo." He then extended his arms out and handed me the baby. "Here. She's yours to take."

The gesture moved me to the core, and even though it didn't work out for us to take the baby to the States, I never forgot the emotion that swept through me at that moment. Thinking about it now, I let out a long sigh. *Whatever happened to the special love we shared? It was gone!*

The chilly weather today motivated me to make a pot of hot chocolate for the men. I stuffed some miniature marshmallows into my pocket to sprinkle on top when I poured their drinks. After removing hot cookies from the oven, I put them onto a large tray to carry down to the cubicle.

Today the team worked on 1 Corinthians 15:35-49 which concerns our glorious, future bodies, the ones we will have in heaven. When I approached the building, I was surprised not to see any of the committee members outside in the sun trying to keep warm. Then, when I reached the door and called out, no one inside responded. *This is unusual,* I thought. Carefully, I balanced the tray on one arm and turned the door knob with my free hand.

"But, how will dead people be brought back to life?" I heard Aparihi asking Jim as I stepped quietly into the room. Six men stared hard at Jim, captivated. "Aren't their bodies already rotten? How will the flesh be put back onto their bones?"

Soundlessly, I set the tray down on a side table, wondering why no one jumped up to help. Normally, any interruption to take a break was welcomed. Today, however, everyone remained seated with their eyes fastened on Jim.

I heard Joshua speaking: "Will our bodies look the same? Or will our new bodies look so different in heaven that no one will recognize us?"

All eyes focused on Joshua as he continued: "Verse 42 says our earthly bodies that die are *different* from the bodies we'll have when we come back to life again. What I want to know is, when my children see me in heaven, will they know it's me ... not someone else?"

The room grew silent waiting for Jim's answer.

"Yes!" Jim stated emphatically, and everyone breathed out a sigh of relief mixed with great jubilation.

"Praise God!" Pastor Ivan blurted out. Then to Jim he said, "We always thought that when we got to heaven, nobody would know who we were."

"Why would you think that?" Jim asked, surprised by this admission.

"Because the Bible says that when we die, we'll get new bodies. We always thought that they would be different from the ones we have on earth, and that no one would recognize us in heaven."

"Well, let's take a minute and look at Jesus after He was raised from the dead," Jim instructed. "The Bible says that when we see Jesus, *we'll be like Him.* So let's see what He looked like after He died and rose again. Everybody, look up John 20:16."

The cubicle had grown so quiet that the swishing of pages seemed loud. *Were they even aware that I had come? Didn't they smell the cookies?* I stared at their captivated faces, eyes riveted on Jim — their teacher was about to provide an answer from God's Word to a question that had burdened their hearts for years.

Reading from the passage Jim continued: "Jesus said to her, 'Mary!' She turned toward him and exclaimed, 'Teacher!'"

"What does this tell us?" Jim asked, wanting the men to participate. Chululu responded boldly: "Mary heard Jesus say her name and knew immediately it was Him." I leaned back against the wall and saw Pastor Ivan wipe a tear from his eye.

"That's right," Jim affirmed. "And so from this passage we know that after the Resurrection, the voice of Jesus was the same. Mary didn't have to see Him, she knew who He was just by hearing Him speak her name."

"Hallelujah!" Pastor Ivan said, overjoyed to know that our voices will remain the same, and that we will be recognized through speaking. The others added their hallelujahs to Ivan's.

"Now let's check and see what His body looked like," Jim continued. "Look further down in the chapter where Jesus appears suddenly to His disciples," Jim directed. "Isoro, read verse 19."

As Isoro read, the men grew ecstatic, poking each other with their elbows and grinning widely. With new eyes they envisioned what had taken place the day Jesus stood among His disciples in the secret room. They tried to imagine the joy that filled the hearts of the disciples upon seeing their Lord.

"Next," Jim continued, "turn in your Bibles to Matthew 17:1-4."

As unobtrusively as possible, I poured hot water into the chocolate mixture and, after quietly stirring each cup, dropped marshmallows on top. "Peter, James and his brother John went to the top of a high hill with Jesus," Jim continued. "Then who came?"

"Moses and Elijah!" Poki replied.

"Did the disciples know who they were?" Jim asked.

"Yes," Joshua replied, and all the men agreed.

"How did the disciples know who Moses and Elijah were? Did Jesus introduce the two men to them?"

The light was beginning to dawn. "Moses and Elijah were dead long before the disciples were born. How did they know them?"

The eyes of the men pierced into Jim, waiting anxiously to hear how the disciples could possibly have known two dead people whom they'd never met.

"God *revealed* it to them," Jim explained. "They didn't need to be introduced. The apostles knew these two men instinctively. And in the same way we will know people we haven't met, and they will know us when we have our new bodies."

By this time the men were so overcome with joy they stood up and shook hands with each other. "Praise God! Hallelujah!" they greeted with each handshake.

I had never seen a group of more joyous men, and decided that now would be a good time to leave and get back home to my work. What did it matter if the cookies were no longer warm? So what if the marshmallows didn't melt on top of the hot chocolate? I could tell these men were savoring something far sweeter.

As noiselessly as possible, I backed out of the cubicle and closed the door behind me. "Hallelujah!" I heard Isoro exclaim loudly as I headed towards home. With the voices of the men praising God in my mind, I walked up the hill feeling an awe for the Lord I had never felt before. God had given each committee member an overwhelming happiness that only He could give. And the source of this joy was His Word. I saw it today with my own eyes. God's Word is living. And it's alive in the Managalasi language.

I hadn't gone far when I heard their familiar voices shouting. I turned around and looked down toward the cubicle. The door flew open. Then, one by one, each team member emerged shouting, whooping and cheering. The hullabaloo brought other translators and their helpers out of their cubicles to see what the racket was all about.

Stunned, I watched our sophisticated pastors and elders run around the entire building like crazy men. "Praise God! All glory to God! Thank you, Lord Jesus!" they shouted over and over, skipping, hopping and jumping. Even Joshua, though he didn't join in the running or shouting, wore a broad smile as he stepped outside the cubicle. He talked with the translation helper who worked in the room next to ours, explaining what had happened to bring on the ruckus.

Other translators emerged from their cubicles to find Jim and inquire about the uproarious behavior. All the while the men continued to run around the building, turning circles and leaping as they praised and thanked God. They didn't care how many people gaped at them as they carried on without restraint—their burden was lifted forever. Let the whole world know!

Could this have been how King David felt when he brought the Ark back to Jerusalem? When he danced in the streets with all his might before the Lord? He didn't care what others thought. What mattered was that he could express his utter joy to God in thanks and praise. It was a mindless kind of joy that only a child of God could possess.

It was exactly what the men were doing this very moment. They, too, as happy as King David, jubilantly celebrated their God.

"O Lord, You are my God; I will exalt You and praise Your name,

for in perfect faithfulness You have done marvelous things, things planned long ago." Isaiah 25:1 (NIV)

"Oo Natohwe A nuni Godia. Na A taarorahe Oni iha unama ahasirivu. Oni mamaa vajijino teamanama para'eme uneunecha mavarasa'ina vehunijija nitama amairiaramana."
Aisea 25:1

Chapter 16

The Chains Fall Off

I heard Jim's footsteps coming up the front steps. I glanced at the clock: 11:30 a.m. I was sitting at the computer concentrating on entering corrections into the text when he walked into the study. "Boy, you're really early for lunch today!" I said, surprised.

Wasting no time, he blurted out, "Joshua sits in the cubicle with us, but stares off into space like he's in a different world. He doesn't take part in the discussions or offer suggestions to help make changes. His obvious lack of participation is affecting the whole committee. Something is bothering him, but I don't know what."

Seeing how disturbed Jim was, I tried to think of something encouraging to say. Nothing came to mind. "Yeah, I know," I uttered, lamely.

"Well, I think there's something *you* can do to help," he declared.

"Like what?" I asked. A feeling of impending doom passed over me.

"Would you work with Joshua here at home? There's a lot of checking you could do that would help us."

My heart dropped. How would I get my typing work done if I had to work all day with Joshua? Besides, he was different now. The relationship we enjoyed in previous years was gone. *Completely gone.* Dismally, I stared back at Jim and said nothing.

"For a start," he continued, "you could read through the changes the committee has been making and get his input. Make sure the grammar is correct, check for clarity, things like that.

"If it's just the two of you working one-on-one, Joshua may apply himself and respond. I've tried everything I know to do to get him to participate. Now it's up to you!"

After Jim left, I continued sitting at the table sipping lukewarm coffee. Thoughts of working with Joshua depressed me. Instead of forgiving him like I knew I should, I grew more angry at him for causing these problems — problems Jim didn't need at this critical time.

Uneasily, I wondered, *Between Joshua behaving badly and my wrong attitude, would God continue to bless us and the work we're doing as He had in the past?*

Later that afternoon, my friend Lois Vincent stopped in for a visit. Like me, Lois was from New Jersey. We met at Ukarumpa in 1962 and have remained like sisters ever since. Lois walked up and down the hills at Ukarumpa every afternoon for exercise. Her route took her past our house and, if time permitted, she'd drop in. Her visits brought encouragement mixed with laughter, and, by the time she left, I felt uplifted.

Today, I welcomed my sister-friend in and unburdened my heart to her, not leaving out any details. Finally I said,

"I begin working with Joshua tomorrow, mainly to remove the tension he's creating in the cubicle," I explained. "This is the last resort. If it doesn't work, Jim will book a flight and send him back to Numba."

My friend's deep concern showed on her face. She sat quietly in the dining room for a moment while I poured her a cup of tea. Quickly, I fixed coffee for myself and joined her at the table.

Without wasting a moment, she began with: "I know how hard it is to forgive, so I'll go home and pray for you. I'm going to ask our Father, Jesus and the Holy Spirit to bring that release and joy to you and Jim that will come with forgiving Joshua."

This was not the answer I expected, and her words disturbed me. Yet, hadn't God already planted seeds in my heart to forgive Joshua? Was God now speaking audibly to me through my friend?

"Joshua's not only hurting you and Jim," she went on, taking a sip of tea, "he's hurting Jesus, his Savior.

"I love the story of the Prodigal Son. And Jesus' instructions to forgive seventy-times-seven helps me, too," she added, and downed the last swallow of tea.

"Thanks, Lo," I replied, feeling unsettled. "I believe your words are what the Lord wanted me to hear right now."

She stood to leave and gave me a quick hug. "Don't worry, my friend," she urged. "God is blessing you and the work of your hands. Release Joshua with your forgiveness, and just be yourself when you work with him tomorrow."

She picked up her cup and took it to the sink. "Remember, love covers all, and it performs miracles!"

I watched her descend the porch steps. When she reached the bottom step, she turned and added, "As I pray for you, please pray for me to be forgiving, too."

"Sure thing!" I called out after her as she walked quickly down the sidewalk to the dirt road. She looked back at me with a grin. "Peace!" she yelled and took off at her usual brisk pace.

I went into the bedroom and picked up my Bible. Opening to Colossians I searched for the verse that would confirm Lois' advice. Yep, there it was in verse 13 of chapter three — "Even as Christ forgave you, so you also *must* do." It came as no surprise. I knew all along I should forgive Joshua. And clearly it was no suggestion from the Lord, but a definite command for His children to forgive.

After breakfast the next morning, Jim pulled the first four chapters of 2 Corinthians out of his briefcase. "Read these over with Joshua," he said. "See if he has anything further to add or take away."

I downed the last bit of coffee and reached for the chapters. "Okay." I replied. "I'll try my best, but I can't promise anything."

"Don't worry about it, just keeping Joshua occupied here will be a help."

"What if he sits in silence here like he's been doing down in the cubicle?"

"Oh, you'll think of something," Jim replied with a confidence I was far from feeling, then he headed for the door.

With the pressure of doing computer corrections off my back, I relaxed. As I sat thinking about the situation, I knew in my spirit that working with Joshua was God's plan for me.

The Lord had already answered prayer as my previous bad feelings were gone! *Lois must have prayed hard and long for me.* Even more surprising to me was that I actually looked forward to going over the chapters with him. Yes, I hoped to correct any errors, but beyond that, I was trusting God to help me forgive Joshua and restore our relationship.

Jupo arrived from her sleeping quarters promptly at 8:00 a.m. She entered in through the back door via the laundry room, and into the dining room. "The sweet potatoes in the storage bin are going bad," she reported. "If you don't eat them soon, they'll rot."

"Bring them in and peel them all," I said. "The translation team is coming for supper, they'll help us eat them."

"What else should I cook? Rice? Bread? Cake?"

"We'll eat rice, too. And you know everyone will be upset if we don't eat cake, so choose the cake you like, and bake that one." She smiled back at me with a look of understanding and proceeded to fetch the sweet potatoes.

Forty-five minutes had gone by and no Joshua. Just as I was beginning to think he wouldn't show up, I heard a knock on the front door. With it came relief and anticipation for what the Lord was going to do for us.

I pulled the door open and gave a cheerful, "Joshua, ese!" He was unprepared for my exuberant greeting and stared at me with a slightly stunned look.

Then, avoiding my glance, he came inside. "Jaki, ese," he replied without enthusiasm.

"Wait a minute while I get the chapters Jim wants us to check," I said, using the warmest tone I could muster.

Jupo stood at the kitchen counter mixing up a chocolate cake. "Amo (father), ese," she greeted. While they talked, I noticed the sweet potatoes were peeled, cut up and in the pot ready to be cooked; the rice was washed and on the stove with a package of dried onion soup floating on top of the water; dough for bread rolls was rising by the window. Supper was half prepared and it wasn't even time for morning tea.

How would I work eight hours and then feed supper to nine people without Jupo? I asked myself, feeling thankful for her expert help.

When I returned with the chapters, Joshua asked, "Did you get a John Wayne movie for us to watch tonight?"

"Yes," I answered, smiling. "Jim picked it up last night." Joshua followed me to the dining room table where we both sat down. The dog PK trotted over and settled under the table by my feet. Quickly, I laid page one on the table in front of Joshua and explained what we would be doing.

"I'll read each verse while you listen carefully and tell me if something doesn't sound correct."

"Okay," he said, his mood light.

"First, let's pray. Would you pray?"

"You can pray," he said, matter-of-factly.

Praying in Managalasi was difficult for me, but I persevered. First I prayed for God's guidance, giving thanks for Joshua's help, and finally asking for His blessing as we worked together.

Then we began reading the translated Scripture and eagerly discussed each verse. In no time he was calling me "Wato" (mother) again. Silently, I gave thanks to God. The light that shone from Joshua's eyes told me he was enjoying our session. Jupo brought us coffee with cookies. Immediately, I broke a cookie in half and slipped a half under the table for PK.

Joshua gave me a startled glance. "You shouldn't waste good food on the dog!" he scolded. "He can eat sweet potatoes later."

"But PK's my baby," I pointed out playfully. "I have no other children here, so I have to take care of PK and keep him a happy dog," I explained. Joshua looked at Jupo and shook his head. Then, the three of us took a break together, munching on warm cookies, drinking coffee and laughing. And the laughter felt good.

When Jim got home for lunch at 1:00 p.m., I told him the good news. "It feels like old times—like nothing's wrong between us." With joy, I showed him the changes we made.

"Great! This is just what I prayed for!" The relief on Jim's face was unmistakable. "I've got to check your changes with the committee," he told me and put the corrected pages into his briefcase. "Just keep doing what you're doing," he encouraged, and went back after lunch to the cubicle for the afternoon session.

At 1:30 p.m., Joshua and I resumed work. It wasn't long before the energy we felt during the morning session faded. Jupo wouldn't be coming to work this afternoon, so I got up to make coffee. Then we pushed ourselves to finish another chapter.

"Wato, I'm going home to shower now," Joshua informed me, standing up and stretching.

"Okay, tell the others to come promptly at 6:30 tonight." Then, feeling mischievous, I added: "If they're late, they won't get any chocolate cake!" Joshua's smile encouraged me. *Could this be the healing Lois told me she would be praying for?*

After the door closed behind Joshua, I began to pray: *Lord, deliver me from the unforgiveness I had in my heart. And, in Your power, help me to care for Joshua as a beloved son once again.*

I began frying hamburgers, stretching the meat with cracker crumbs so each man could have two burgers instead of one. At exactly 6:05 p.m. the knock came. Without waiting for me to open the door, Chululu walked in. "Jaki, ese!" he said, and the rest followed him in. "Jaki, ese!" each said in turn.

"Ese, ese, ese," I replied, nodding to each man. "It's not 6:30 yet, why are you here so early?"

Without wasting a second, Poki replied, "We were afraid we wouldn't get any chocolate cake, so we hurried." His eyes gleamed with amusement. The other men laughed heartily and took their places at the table. We were off to a good start.

I saw Chululu motion secretly to Jim, and they went into the study. *Hmm, something's up,* I thought. Curiosity got the better of me, so instead of dishing up the food, I dashed into the study after them. As soon as I got there, Jim caught my eye and nodded. "The mystery is solved," he said.

"You mean regarding Joshua's behavior? What's been the problem?"

"It all has to do with his salary," Jim explained while Chululu sat down on the chair at my desk.

Dumbfounded by this unexpected response, I stood there staring from Jim to Chululu, then back to Jim.

"Joshua thought we would pay him the same amount of money for doing translation work as the government paid him for his teaching job."

Without waiting for Jim to finish, Chululu chimed in, "He didn't know there wasn't any money in the translation fund. He thought the churches in America were sending you plenty of money for the translation and that you and Jim were misusing the funds to buy other things. Once I told Joshua that there was no money in the translation fund, he wasn't angry anymore."

I looked at Jim. "When did you find out about this?"

"Just now. Last night Chululu asked Joshua outright what was bothering him, and Joshua told him—he needs more money to pay his daughter Kumari's school bill at the university, but he can't do it on the salary we pay him."

"How much money did you promise him when you hired him?" I asked.

"Well, when he told me he felt God wanted him to work with the translation full time, I didn't say anything about salary. I knew we would have to pay seven or eight men and felt they should all be paid the same amount. There's no way we could pay each checker 700 kina ($350) a month, and that's what Kumari needs for her school bill."

"So that's why he's been acting strangely—he gave up a good-paying job to help us, and now he's in debt," I said slowly, summing up the situation. "If only he had come and talked to us about it." I said wistfully.

Chululu broke into the conversation. "Telling you that he needed more money would have brought him shame," he revealed, disclosing another facet of the culture. Then, without further ado, he got up and went into the dining room to join the others.

"We should go get the food ready," Jim reminded me. "The guys are probably starved."

As we entered the kitchen, my thoughts flew back woefully to the prayer I had prayed only a few hours ago. *"Lord, help me to forget the hurtful things and care for Joshua like a son,"* I had prayed.

Satan is sure working on me full time, I concluded.

Sighing in defeat, I carried a large plate of rice to the table. Jim followed with the hamburger patties. After everyone was seated and settled down, Jim announced, "Let's pray." After asking for God's blessing on the food, the men ate ravenously, talking and joking throughout dinner. Still upset by Joshua's thoughts, my mood did not match theirs.

So soon, Lord? I fretted. *Did You have to test my forgiving Joshua so soon? I failed the test, Lord,* I confessed. "Why, Lord, ... why is it so hard to have faith when you go through hard times — like forgiving people who hurt you? You see my heart, Lord. You know that I want to do Satan's will and stay angry, rather than do Your will and forgive."

After I finished talking to God, I thought about how my negative thinking would stop the flood of light He promised from bursting through: that God worked where there was an attitude of faith. Did that mean He wouldn't love me in the same way?

Lord, please help my lack of faith!

While the men were eating dessert, Jim inserted a video into the machine and called us to come to the living room. The men jumped up from the table; they were about to see their favorite cowboy perform on his horse. Some took their chocolate cake with them to finish eating during the movie. Isoro walked to the couch, noisily licking the last of the frosting from his fingers.

"First we're going to watch the video that our daughter Tanya made when she came back to the village with her husband, Ted." Jim announced, surprising all of us, even me.

"When did Tanya's video arrive?" I asked.

"During our break this afternoon I went to the post office, and there it was."

Before I could say another word, Jim pushed "play" and turned off the lights. The room grew silent as the familiar

sights of the airstrip flashed on with the Managalasi warriors
excitedly surrounding the plane with spears.

Each man leaned forward on their seat so they wouldn't
miss a word. Seeing themselves on TV brought hoots of
laughter. Isoro, dressed as one of the warriors, had red paint
smeared all over his face. Now, sitting on our couch, the
fierce warrior covered his face with both hands to hide his
embarrassment.

Several minutes into Tanya's story, Joshua and his wife
Cracker appeared, standing in front of our village house.
Tanya, with excitement in her voice, announced boldly: "And
the biggest present Mom and Dad received this Christmas
was Joshua's surprise—he told them he felt God leading
him into translation work. He plans to quit his teaching job
to work full time checking the New Testament with Dad."

The room grew so quiet, that if anyone dropped a cake
crumb, it would have sounded like a china plate crashing.
I jerked my head toward Joshua. He cringed noticeably and
sat back in his chair with his eyes shut as he listened to
himself speak.

"I have decided to leave my teaching position and take up
translation work full time," he announced on video. "There
is a need for my people to have God's Word in their own
language."

There it was, out in the open for everyone to witness. The
men, ill at ease, looked away from the screen. Some stared
at the floor. In the silence, I felt the need to go over and
comfort Joshua, but, as if glued to my seat, I couldn't move.

As I pondered the situation, I was amazed to find that
the hurt and resentment I felt before dinner had melted
away completely, and an unexplainable affection for Joshua
overtook me. It didn't matter what he had done, and it
didn't matter what he would do in the future, my heart was

suddenly filled with love and caring for this young man…
our Managalasi son. I knew it was God doing for me what
I could not do for myself.

When the video ended, Jim removed it, and the men began
talking again, remembering jovially Ted and Tanya's visit.
Jim quickly inserted the John Wayne movie. I stole a glance
at Joshua who remained sitting with his eyes shut. A moment
later, the hero's face appeared on the screen, and all the men
cheered. All except Joshua. As events unfolded, the men sat
laughing heartily once again.

Two hours later, the movie ended, and the guys, not wanting to go home, continued to sit around and talk. Joshua sat
silently, looking uncomfortable. Jim stood up and walked
over to him. Reaching through the man's distress, Jim talked
quietly with him. "How much do you owe for Kumari's
school bill?" he asked.

Joshua hesitated awkwardly, then cleared his throat before
mumbling an amount.

"Well, we will help you pay her bill, but I can't tell you
how much we can give until after we receive our financial
statement from Wycliffe. The statements should arrive this
Wednesday."

Joshua glanced at Jim then turned away quickly, nodding
his head repeatedly. As the men began putting on their jack-
ets, I walked over to join Jim and Joshua. Before I could say
anything, Joshua took my hand and shook it, then reached
for Jim's hand and did the same. Jim pumped his hand with
happiness in return. The huge burden both men carried for
months was gone, *the chains of unforgiveness had fallen off.
We had been set free.*

Instinctively, I had my answer — no matter what I did,
God's love for me would never change. His love wasn't based
on my behavior, but stemmed from before I was born, while

I was yet in my mother's womb, He loved me! And it would never change!

Joy lit up the entire room as we said our goodbyes. *Could this be the light God promised would burst forth?* It seemed like the love we felt for Joshua had extended itself to everyone.

God did something powerful, and the end of a difficult situation had come. Love stepped in and filled our hearts, reminding me that God is in control of the universe.

"And let us not lose heart in doing good, for in due time we shall reap if we do not grow weary." Galatians 6:9 (NASB)

"Roe nu mamaiji vehunijaho paucha'asa'avara. Ijihuni maijaho vea nimaa ro ape'eje a pasena'eje ve'amajaho ijihuni eha apehuna." Karesia 6:9

A
Photo Gallery

To the left of the village stands the Ese Bible Institute. The school continues to transform lives throughout the Managalasi plateau.

After growing up in the concrete jungle of Newark, NJ, my appreciation for God's majestic scenery went down deep.

Living in an isolated village requires us to travel in a small plane.

Getting dangerous cargo, like gas and kerosene, required the helicopter.

Young people carrying cargo from the airstrip to our house in
Numba Village

The road leading up to Numba village.

Some of the children brought us a gift — a flying fox.

Kwaare brings a hornbill to keep for a pet.

Before becoming believers, the Managalasis never left their houses after dark for fear of the spirits.

Food is cooked in large pots over open fires.

Pigs are kept tied to prevent their rooting up gardens.

A typical bride price included plenty of woven mats, cutlery, dishes and money taped to a bamboo.

Delicious, fresh coconut provides flavor to garden food.

Chululu's son Ahausa, a talented builder, helped build our house, the church and the Bible School.

"If you're not lazy and come to class every day, you will learn to read and write," I promise the men.

Kirija, a faithful helper, checks language work.

In the beginning days, Jaki often accompanied Sonalu to the river and learned much about the culture and language.

Girls learn to help with family chores at an early age.

A hand-made ball made from the sponge-like core of a tree provides village fun for children.

Weaving a bamboo wall.

Friends were happy to go to the river to fetch our drinking water.

Hwi'ura, Isoro's older brother, was always ready to help when and wherever needed.

Platforms are built to dry coffee beans.

Preparing coffee to sell is a labor shared by husbands and wives.

Sinaja, one of our oldest friends, learned to read and write her language.

Gene Cunningham teaches the very first course to 48 students: "I never taught a group of more hungry men for the Word of God than these right here in Numba Village.

Jim congratulates the oldest student to graduate EBI.

Virginia gets the food prepared for students to come and eat.

The Wind House, where students gather for meals.

Chululu, an enthusiastic teacher, loves to teach God's Word.

Chululu baptizes new believers.

Jim teaches about the end times in Dea, Gilbert's village.

Because of the Ese Bible Institute, the churches now work together.

Ese Bible Institute class in session.

Nan and Desiree with Manuel, the head of the Sunday School Department. "I prayed for 15 years that God would send help."

Desiree hikes several hours to reach children who don't have opportunities to hear the Word.

Boys and girls proudly hold up their work for the teacher.

Chululu has helped Jim since the beginning of our ministry in 1962.

Chapter 17

A Visit With Old Friends

A few months after we had gone back to the village, we learned that our dear friends Al and Ruth Roberts would be coming to visit us in Papua New Guinea. At last they would meet the Managalasi people for whom they had prayed for over three decades. Thoughts of their soon arrival excited me daily.

One concern, however, was that our food supplies were running low. Fortunately, we had a radio conversation scheduled today with Bob and Ruth Merz. Every time I thought about it, I'd add something new to the grocery list. Al and Ruth's coming provided us with an opportunity to order extra goodies from the Ukarumpa store, like fresh meat, cokes and cake mixes, beside the essentials, like sugar and flour.

I glanced at the clock above the kitchen window—10:00 a.m.—15 minutes to go. In anticipation, I turned on the two-way radio and called in—*just in case they came up early*. The whistling noises and static emitted from the radio were beyond belief. "We'll never get through today," I remarked dismally to Jim who sat at the table trying to fix Isoro's rusty lantern.

"Doesn't sound like it," Jim agreed. "Just wait a few minutes and try calling in again."

165

At 8:10 p.m. I put the mouthpiece to my lips: "Mike Oscar, Mike Oscar, this is Sierra Oscar standing by. Are you reading me?"

No response. *Oh no,* I thought, beginning to lose hope. *How will I get my goodies from the store if Bob and Ruth forgot about our radio sched? And our mail! It's been five weeks since we received news from home!*

Promptly at 8:15 Bob's voice rang out: "Sierra Oscar, Sierra Oscar, this is Mike Oscar standing by."

I let out a huge sigh of relief. "Reading you loud and clear!" I responded cheerfully. Bob's voice was as clear as a bell. The whistling noises had disappeared!

"Tell us how things are going for you out there," Ruth chimed in.

We chatted with these friends for half an hour — moments of pure bliss, thanks to the two-way radio. Ruth took down my list of eleven items, plus the Cokes and chocolate bars. Bob took Jim's order for blackboards and medicine.

After saying our goodbyes, I asked Jim: "Do you think the clinic will send the penicillin we need to treat all the people who have pneumonia?"

"I don't know," Jim replied slowly. "We didn't give much notice. Bob and Ruth will have to go directly to the clinic from the Radio Shack to see about it."

"Some of the older people will die without it," I said, verbalizing what Jim already knew and feared.

The next morning Jim and I scurried through the breakfast

routine and headed immediately for the airstrip to greet the Roberts. A crowd of village people tagged along, anxious to see this American couple who had prayed for them for the past 35 years.

Jupo carried bottles of water and a large container of pineapple chunks in the stringbag that suspended from her head. By the time we reached Sila Airstrip I was reeling with exhaustion from the heat. It was that last hill to the top of the airstrip that always did me in. Jupo noted my shortness of breath and handed me a bottle of water. "Thank you," I said gratefully, unscrewed the lid, tilted back my head and drank greedily.

Our friendship with Al and Ruth stemmed back to the mid '50's. Ruth and I had graduated from Nutley High School in New Jersey together, then went on to Northeastern Bible Institute to study God's Word.

In 1962, the week before we boarded the ship to Papua New Guinea, Al and Ruth hosted us in their home near San Francisco. During our stay, we visited Travis Air Force Base where Al was an Air Force pilot. There, Lieutenant Roberts purchased some equipment we would need to live in the isolated area on a mountain top. How grateful we were for their help in getting us started.

"The plane is coming," Jupo informed me. I stopped gulping long enough to listen. Sure enough, off in the far distance came the sound of an engine. I felt a wave of goose bumps move down my arms. Jim began signaling to the crowd of spectators to back off the airstrip and stand behind the cones. We watched the Cessna circle around and land at the bottom of the grassy strip, then taxi up to the top.

As soon as Al and Ruth caught sight of us waving frantically, their faces lit up with smiles. The pilot got out quickly and walked around the aircraft to open the door for the passengers. That's when it struck me how incredible it seemed for Ruth and me to meet again on this isolated airstrip 13,000 miles from home. It was like a dream.

Amidst our hugs and tears, Ruth wiped the perspiration from her brow almost constantly. Al, a military man, withstood the intense middle-of-the-day heat well, but it affected Ruth immediately.

Jim's voice broke into our happy chatter. "You and Ruth better start moving," he urged. "You know how long it takes to hike to the village."

I cringed as I thought about the trek up and down the hills. I knew the hike would be tough on Ruth. Yet, as we began our journey, she chatted non-stop, as if nothing were out of the ordinary. Happiness bubbled inside me as our minds raced with memories from both high school and Bible school days.

Jupo, carrying Ruth's suitcase, went on ahead to open the house and start putting lunch on the table. Moments later Jim and Al passed us, walking briskly with some of the men who carried boxes of food. When I saw Aparihi's youngest brother, Jiveta balancing a case of coke on his shoulder, I ejected a happy sigh of relief. Jiveta saw my face light up and flashed back a knowing smile. Jiveta was our faithful helper who came to the house every night and filled our refrigerater with kerosine. Now, as he passed us on the trail, he gave me a big smile. He knew how much I loved Coke.

"Lunch will be on the table waiting for you … if you ever get home," Jim called back.

At that moment, Ruth and I couldn't have cared less how long it took us to get home. We were enjoying ourselves too much strolling along, talking and eating juicy pineapple. *Papua New Guinea must produce the sweetest, best-tasting pineapple in the world,* I thought to myself, and, in unladylike fashion, I wiped my mouth and chin on my shirtsleeve.

During our walk home, Ruth only stopped twice to rest. Knowing how uncomfortable she must have felt, I marveled at her perseverance to keep pushing on.

It was great to finally reach home and find lunch on the table ready and waiting.

The Store at Ukarumpa where our supplies are ordered and sent out to us in the village.

"I pray that the fellowship of your faith may become effective through the knowledge of every good thing which is in you for Christ's sake." Philemon 1:6 (NASB)

"Nara siporua ka'ene 'ojujaho raka ka'ene ara nimaa ronuji ea 'aho'a 'wara'amajaho maa rukina'e rehuna. 'Ene Keriso Oni jihuna'e henaka mapoka mamaaka oni vaji navujaho roe maa rukina rehuna." Pairimani 1:6

Chapter 18

Trading Marks

The day after the Roberts arrived, Al asked about meeting Marija, the former village chief. Al wanted to hear Marija's stories about running for the Allied troops during WWII. Jim would be the interpreter.

Al, Jim and I walked the short distance to the village, while Chululu took Ruth on a tour to one of the nearby gardens. "I want to see how they grow their food!" Ruth called out to us as she trailed after Chululu. Several children tagged along with them.

When we arrived at Marija's house, I was relieved to find him sitting on the porch looking well. Lately, he'd been coming to the house with a deep, rasping cough that shook him to the core. At night he struggled with chest pain. Now, as I observed him sitting comfortably waiting for us, I could see that the medicine was helping.

When Marija saw us approaching, he stood up slowly and reached out to shake our hands.

"Ese!" Al greeted enthusiastically, gripping the chief's hand. After we all shook hands we sat down together on the steps of Marija's house. Al and my village father then went on to discuss at length the military strategies used in Papua New Guinea. Finally, after an hour, they wore the subject out. Jim then switched gears and began to describe how Marija had met John Glenn when the senator and astronaut had come to visit Numba Village. First, Jim shared his thoughts on that visit.

"John and Annie Glenn, along with a delegation of 23 others, flew from Washington, D.C. to our village," Jim began. "I met the group in Port Moresby and flew with them to Sila Airstrip. When they deplaned, I wondered why no one from our village had come to welcome this important group of visitors. Surely the Managalasis had received my notice in plenty of time! I searched in every direction for signs of life, but all was quiet. I not only felt disappointed, but a little embarrassed too.

"I led the group from the airstrip to the village. Imagine my shock as we arrived in Numba and found the village empty. *Where was everybody?* I wondered.

"Suddenly, quick as lightening, the village men came rushing towards us from the underbrush. Red-faced warriors bolted out from behind the trees and bushes yelling war cries, their spears poised, ready for attack!

"The group from Washington looked terrified. They froze, as if waiting for the thrust of the spear to pierce their bodies. One fierce-looking guy grabbed the senator by the shoulder, turned him around and brought his spear to within inches of his chest. Then, instantly, his warrior-like expression changed, and he started laughing!

"'Ese,' he greeted, signaling the other warriors to do likewise. The atmosphere changed immediately, and the would-be attackers shook hands with the visitors. 'Ese! Ese!' they said, welcoming them with broad smiles. Then others poured down from their houses and ran to join the visitors.

"Then it hit me—*everybody was in on it!*" Jim revealed to Al. "I wasn't quite sure what to say to Senator Glenn. I hemmed and hawed at first, then finally explained: 'The men wanted to show you how they attacked their enemies during tribal warfare. Did they frighten you?'

"'I'm afraid so,'" admitted the senator. 'After all, *they* knew they weren't going to spear me, but I didn't.'"

Al and Jim both laughed together, and Jim went on with his story:

"After the initial shock was over, I took the visitors to our house where they were able to wash up and totally relax with a cool drink and some Oreo cookies. Jupo and Cookie served the sweet pineapple, papaya and mangos they had cut up earlier and put in the fridge to stay cool. Then Cookie turned on the stove to cook yams and taros so the guests could sample their garden vegetables.

"Two hours later, the group left our house and gathered together at the lower part of the village where a make-shift platform was set up. The village people spread out banana leaves for the delegation to sit down on directly in front of the platform, and the villagers sat behind them. Everyone wanted to hear what the senator had accomplished in outer space. Poki interpreted the senator's words to the Numba people.

"First, Senator Glenn stood facing Marija as leader to leader. He explained about his flight in space in the simplest terms possible to the chief. When he had finished, Marija remained unmoved. To the chief's thinking, Americans were 'super human beings' and could do anything, whether it be flying rockets in space or walking on the moon.

"When it was Marija's turn to speak, the unschooled chief told the senator of his coming to faith in Jesus. 'After we received God's Word in our language, I learned how much God loved me, and sent His Son Jesus to die for my sins. I'm now His son,' Marija admitted boldly to John Glenn.

"After hearing Marija's story, Senator Glenn took off the

bicentennial medal President Kennedy had awarded him.

'What your chief just told me is more important than anything I ever did in space,' the senator proclaimed to the audience of more than 400 people. 'Annie and I have a Bible on our coffee table at home,' he added, 'and we read it together every night.'

"With those words he placed the medal from the president around Marija's neck. The village chief reciprocated by removing the shell necklace he wore and handed it to the senator. The necklace had been passed down through generations to each succeeding village chief. The exchange represented 'trading their marks.'

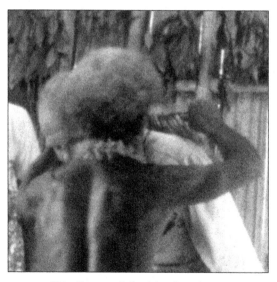

"Trading Marks" with John Glenn.

"All too soon the delegation prepared for the hike to the airstrip and their flight back to Port Moresby. The weather had cooled a bit, making the return hike to the airstrip more bearable.

"Just before getting onto the plane, Senator Glenn turned

to me and said: 'Seeing this place, meeting these people and listening to this chief today has been one of the most educational experiences of my life.'"

"I learned that God sent Jesus to die for me. I'm now His son," Marija admitted boldly to Senator Glenn.

"If anyone is ashamed of Me and My words in this adulterous and sinful generation, the Son of Man will be ashamed of him when he comes in his Father's glory with the holy angels."
Mark 8:38 (NIV)

"Ea mapoka ka'ene iviamaa iki hijukija Godi pataarohe 'ee sisea 'unama ani ani veji'i hiju. Ea irara Nuni jihuna'e Na pataarorihe 'ee Nuni ira pataaro'amajaho vea ka'ene Ema Puni Harihijara 'ona oji'ina arimaa 'ee Amoni haniji'iniji'i ro'amajaho Hu 'u'o pataarohuna." Maka 8:38

Chapter 19

Laying Up Treasure

One night after supper Al and Ruth marveled as they watched Jupo type my women's notes for the upcoming meeting. "She can type faster than I can!" Ruth blurted out.

"Where did she learn to use a computer?" Al asked, looking impressed.

Jupo, a remarkable helper and typist.

"Oh, I taught her in my spare time. Jupo is a fast learner, it didn't take her long to get the hang of it. Learning to cup her hands over the keys on the home row was the hardest thing for her to master. But, like everything else, she hung in there and conquered the problem. Now, I admit, she really does type as fast as I do."

"Wow," Ruth exclaimed. "Did she help you type any of the translation?"

"Yes! That was the main reason I taught her to type. The time and effort I put into teaching her has paid off in more ways than one.

"The most beneficial thing is that Jupo proofreads as she types. Several times she's come up with corrections ... things like verbs that should have been in the plural form, and other errors we overlooked. The Committee started to complain that Jupo was giving them too much extra work with all her corrections to check.

"Another thing, once the village people found out about Jupo being able to type, they all wanted to learn. Unfortunately, I only have one computer."

"If you had some typewriters, would you teach others, too?" Al asked pointedly.

"Well ... I hadn't thought about it ...," I stammered. "But, probably."

On Sunday morning, promptly at 10:00, one of the men began blowing the conch shell announcing that the church service was about to begin. Al and Ruth went on ahead. When they reached the church, they made their way down to the second row and sat on a sawn log that served as a bench. The people were already singing a hymn. The eyes of the two visitors swept over the congregation observing the people they had prayed for since 1962. These people, who once lived in darkness, were now singing hymns of praise to the Savior. Overcome with emotion, Al and Ruth wiped away tears of joy, giving thanks and praise to God throughout the entire song service.

When the song service ended, Pastor Ivan stood and, with his Managalasi New Testament under his arm, went forward to preach the message. Although Al and Ruth couldn't understand a word, they continued to weep—the answers to their prayers of more than three decades had now become sight.

After the service ended, Jim and I stood talking with friends at the rear of the church. Out of the corner of my eye I watched Al and Ruth shake hands with as many people as possible. Later we walked over to join them.

"This is the best investment we've ever made," Al said, his eyes still moist. "God has answered our prayers beyond what we expected. We started out with just a list of names on paper. Today those names have been transformed into faces right before our eyes!"

Al hesitated, and took a few minutes to collect his thoughts. "Talk about a 'return on an investment,'" he said finally, "there is no comparison in the world of finance."

"Do not store up for yourselves treasures on earth where moth and rust destroy, and where thieves break in and steal. But store up for yourselves treasures in heaven where moth and rust do not destroy, and where thieves do not break in and steal." Matthew 6:19–20 (NIV)

"'Ene uneunecha ka'ene mamaijija ikaho mwe'a paahuma irechama hi'avara. Ijihuni maijaho soapo ine 'ee kapurapo 'uhusame 'ee ea ka'ene nesa apeji'inijipo nesi tirasame aruma va'e nesi 'ekahuna. 'Enakune joni uneunecha maa kajija kahino akupa 'ahi ahume irechava na'avara. 'Ejakame soa 'ee kapura pa'uhusame 'ee ea nesa pa'ekahuna." Matiu 6:19, 20

Chapter 20

Arrival of the Typewriters

The one-week visit sped by all too quickly, and the Roberts were on their way back to Huntley, Illinois. After they arrived home, their enthusiasm for helping the Managalasi people infected the entire Sunday School at Village Church of Barrington. Class members collected twenty-five typewriters with extra ribbons and shipped them overseas. Those typewriters would be arriving via helicopter today, one month later.

Almost everyone in the village showed up to watch the whirly bird land. The grassy area to the right of our house served as a perfect landing pad. Although I had ridden in the helicopter many times, watching it descend or lift off always thrilled me. Now we heard the buzz of the engine coming in the distance.

"The helicopter is coming! The helicopter is coming!" children squealed, jumping up and down. My eyes followed their outstretched arms pointing toward the mountains. I caught sight of the giant bird approaching between two mountain peaks. Two 44-gallon drums dangled from slings beneath the aircraft. One was filled with gasoline for the generator, and the other contained kerosene for our refrigerator and lamps. All who had gathered, both young and old, erupted in cheers.

Pilot Alan Van Doren skillfully descended to just above the grassy patch, then guided the aircraft so that the 44-gallon drums gently touched down onto the grass. Jim waited for the aircraft to steady itself overhead.

"Poki!" Jim called out. "You and Jon Mari untie the drums and roll them under the house!"

The helicopter hovered above as the men untied the drums. Then Jim quickly appointed other young men to help roll both drums safely beneath our house for storage until we needed fuel.

Alan then descended and landed on the grassy patch. "Hey there! How ya doin?" Alan greeted joyfully as he climbed down from the aircraft.

"We're doin' okay," Jim replied, returning the smile. "Good to see you!"

The men shook hands and Alan greeted me with a hug. He then quickly unlocked the aircraft and unloaded the typewriters, handing each to Jim who in turn handed them to the men standing in back of him.

"Just set them on the grass for now," Jim instructed the men.

Lastly, Alan held up the mailbag with a big grin.

"Waiting for this by any chance?" he teased, dangling the red cloth bag in front of my face.

"You bet!" I replied, snatching it out of his hand.

Pilots knew what made translators happiest. When you lived in an isolated village, aircraft days were without a doubt the most exciting days. Without pilots to deliver news from home and food items like fresh meat, butter, sugar and flour, life would be a lot more difficult. We praised the Lord often for each and every pilot.

Jim and Alan talked for a few minutes, and then Alan climbed back into the cockpit. Seconds after the engines started, the blades above were whirling. By this time, everyone in the village had arrived to watch the magical machine lift off. The blades whirled faster and faster, and the chopper rose. It flew over the church, whipping the palm trees frantically. We all watched as it whirly-birded up into the blaring blue sky and disappeared over the mountains.

Ahause and Chris made several trips carrying the typewriters into the 20 x 30 foot classroom and setting them on the desks. When Jim initially prepared the room for literacy classes, he nailed sheets of plywood down onto bamboo poles for desks. Each desk would accommodate three students. Jim's next job would be to examine each typewriter to make sure it worked properly. This wouldn't be hard to do since Al Roberts had already hired someone in Chicago to check all the typewriters and fix anything that needed fixing. Al thought of everything.

Typing classes were to begin in two weeks. The notice I posted on our front porch brought an overwhelming response. More than 25 eager men and women verbally expressed interest to us. Jim and I faced hard decisions in choosing only 25. Perhaps we would anger some people, or maybe lose friends as a result of these decisions.

Lord, show me how to handle this, I prayed. Soon after asking for God's help, the thought occurred to me: *Have each student fill out an application!*

Yes! An application would help narrow down the list! I'll ask how they will use their new typing skill. The answer to this question would help me choose. *Thank You, Lord.*

Several men came that day and handed me their applications. Suaga, a young man from another village sat down and fixed his eyes intently on me. I checked his application first:

The first question read: *Why do you want to learn to type?*

Suaga's answer: *to know how to typing a whiter.*

The next question: *How will you use your typing skill?*

Answer: *By looking at the letters on the typing whiter.*

I stopped reading and searched frantically in my mind for a kind way to inform Suaga he would not be able to take the class.

Jim and I found that most applicants wanted to learn to type in order to keep better records for their businesses. Some of the girls were secretaries at government stations and longed to learn the skill.

Magunda, Chululu's son-in-law, worked in the Tax Office in Port Moresby and typed with two fingers. He informed us he would be flying home to Numba this afternoon so he could learn to type properly.

Finally, after days of deliberating with Jim, I typed a list of names revealing the fortunate 25 who would begin class on Monday morning. I tacked the list to our front door and walked over to the classroom.

Chris and Ahause were working up a sweat, scrubbing the entire room. The windows sparkled. Jim was still checking typewriters. "The machines are all working great!" he told me happily.

"Good!" I said, then asked: "Would you help me hang this keyboard chart so every student in the room will see it easily?"

Jim nailed the chart up at the front of the classroom in no time; everything was ready. We thanked Chris and Ahause for their hard work, and walked home together. To our surprise, we found Solomon, our next-door neighbor, waiting with his son Manu on our porch. Even though Solomon seldom smiled, he was a kind, likeable man. Manu, however, wore a stern, almost angry expression. His fiery eyes made me uneasy, and I kept my distance.

"Ese, Solomon! Ese, Manu," I greeted, wondering what they could possibly want. Both men coughed and, for the first time, Manu seemed unsure of himself. His eyes averted mine, and he stared into space, waiting for his father to speak.

"Um, er," Solomon hemmed and hawed. "We've been thinking about the class you're going to have on Monday," he stammered. "I want my daughter Natalene to be one of the students."

"We only have space for 25, and all those places are taken," Jim informed him. "It's too late for Natalene to come to this session, but next year there will be another class. She can come then."

Manu's eyes hardened. He sniffed into the air, the cultural way of showing distaste. "Your house is on our land," Manu reminded us in an angry tone. "It's only right that our family members be the first ones to come to your class."

Was he threatening us? I wondered. *If we didn't allow Natalene to attend class, would he force us off his land?* Panic. I hoped Jim would come to the rescue. He did.

"Now wait a minute," Jim said, his tone firm. "Did Natalene fill out an application?"

"No," Solomon admitted. "She lives far away and didn't hear about the classes until she came to visit us today. When I told her, she started crying, so I came to ask you to give her a place in the class."

"Well, if we had another typewriter, she could come to class," Jim reminded him gently, "but all 25 are taken already."

"Tell one of the students he can't come!" Manu demanded.

"No!" Jim said firmly. "That wouldn't be fair to the others who brought us their applications on time."

Jim's mouth had become a grim line. Manu's eyes flashed anger at us, then he spit on the ground.

Solomon stood hunched over, like a man who carried many burdens. "Natalene should have been accepted before Loaka and his wife," he stated without emotion. "They only need *one* typist in their family, not two."

"I must go cook our food," I interrupted, easing the tension a little. "Goodnight." I left the three men standing on the porch and went into the house. In this culture, emotion was far stronger than logic. *So what if Natalene didn't fill out an application — we live on her father's land!*

In a few minutes the lights in the house lit up and I knew Jim had taken the opportunity to leave also and start the generator.

The next morning I saw Natalene sitting next to her mother in church. We exchanged awkward glances before her eyes glazed, and she focused on something in the distance.

I wondered what thoughts were going through her mind at that moment.

"I ask you not to lose heart at my tribulations on your behalf, for they are your glory." Ephesians 3:13 (NASB)

"Ijihuni hahi na ja 'waravujaho nara joni jihuna'e sisei hijujaho ja paki'eje joni oja veje areri paretiama." Epasasi 3:13

Chapter 21

The First Typing Class

On Monday, I woke up before the morning's first hint of light, anxious for the day to begin. I splashed water on my face and dressed quickly. Next, I sat at my desk and read some verses out of Proverbs. Lastly, feeling highly motivated, I jogged to the kitchen to get breakfast on the table.

"Jim!" I called, waking him. "Breakfast is ready!"

When Jim got to the table and saw me putting jelly on my toast, he raised his eyebrows. "What's going on and why are we having breakfast so early?"

"Nothing really," I responded nonchalantly. "It's just that I'm excited about our first typing class and couldn't sleep."

After my last swallow of coffee, I got up from the table and headed for the door. "I'm going to the classroom to make sure I have everything I'll need for the class."

"Mmm, okay," Jim mumbled in reply, and buttered another piece of toast.

Reaching the small building next to our house, I pushed open the creaky door and glanced around inside. The spanking clean room reinforced my mounting anticipation.

Promptly at 8:30 a.m. the students arrived and drifted into the room. Natalene walked in nonchalantly and took a seat in the third row. My mouth dropped open. She noted my look of surprise and looked down at the typewriter in front of her. "Loaka won't be coming," she offered apologetically. "He told me I could have his place and he would come next year."

I nodded back at her wordlessly, concluding that the two households of cousins had worked out their own solution. Knowing that the class would be more beneficial for Natalene than for Loaka, I pushed aside the slow burn creeping up my neck and watched the other students pile into the room. Chattering with excitement, each chose the seat they would use for the next six weeks.

"Welcome to the first typing class in Managalasi history," I greeted enthusiastically, and the room erupted with thunderous applause. When the class finally quieted down, all eyes settled on me.

"First, I'm going to show you how to put paper into the typewriter," I said. "It's important to always use *two* pieces," I instructed, then demonstrated by whipping two pages in with a flick of the wrist. Jon Mari picked up one piece.

"Jon Mari!" I yelled. "*Two* pieces of paper!"

Jon Mari smiled sheepishly as he reached for another piece of paper, keeping one leery eye on me.

"If you don't use two pieces, you will ruin the rubber roller," I explained. Then, pointing to the enlarged chart hanging at the front, I introduced them to the home row. "This is how to hold your hands and fingers on the home row," I said, demonstrating. Then, as if they hadn't seen my hands at all, everyone spread their fingers wide apart and held their hands as stiff as boards.

"No, no! Hold your hands loosely! Keep your fingers rounded, like you're holding a ball." The more I explained, the more I realized my words were useless. It was like they had wooden hands.

A depressing thought came to mind: *For most of their lives these men and women have known only garden work; they'll never be able to train their hands to accomplish a skill like typing. There's no hope for any of them!*

Despondently, I walked up and down the rows, clapping my hands to help them establish a rhythm. Then I began helping each individual posture their hands properly on the keys. Nothing I said helped them relax their fingers. Groaning inwardly, I observed them placing their hands out flat above the keyboard while using their forefingers to hammer the "f" and "j" keys. Helplessly, I let out a tense breath and closed my eyes. *Would I ever persuade them to keep their fingers rounded and on the home row?*

An opportunity to learn to type comes to the Managalasi people.

As I continued circulating among them, a familiar phrase came to mind: "*Practice makes perfect.*" Still, instinctively I knew that producing Managalasi typists would take divine intervention. My strength and enthusiasm were fading fast, but I pushed on until noon before dismissing the class.

"Come back at 8:30 tomorrow morning!" I announced,

secretly hoping they would all go to their gardens and forget about typing. But, to my surprise, not one student moved.

"*You* go and have lunch," one student said. "We're going to stay and keep on practicing."

"Yes," they all agreed, eyes fixed hopefully on me.

"Okay," I managed to say. "I'll come back after lunch and check to see how you're doing." With that I left the room and staggered home.

Cookie had cut up some canned Vienna sausages and mixed them in with a can of beans. The mixture was warming on the stove when I got home. The aroma spread through the kitchen, and it smelled wonderful. I splurged and opened a can of Coke.

"Let's eat!" I called to Jim who was sifting through paperwork in his study. We sat down at the table and made sausage and bean sandwiches with Cookie's delicious home-made rolls. As we ate lunch we could hear the typewriters clicking and the bells ringing from next door in the classroom.

"Well, how did your first day go?" Jim asked with raised eyebrows.

"I think most of them learned how to put paper in their typewriters, but they're hopeless at keeping their hands and fingers curved on the keyboard. I'm ready to quit!"

"It doesn't sound like your students are ready to quit. Why are they still in the classroom?"

"They wanted to stay and practice, so I told them I'd go back after lunch and see how they're doing."

"Why don't you just stay home and rest?" Jim suggested, surprising me. "I won't be working with Joshua this afternoon, so I can check on the students. In fact, I'll go now." He swallowed his last bite of sandwich and stood up. "See ya later," he said, and promptly left the kitchen.

"Thank you!" I called to his retreating back. After he left, I went into the bedroom and stretched out on the bed for a few minutes of therapeutic de-stressing. As I lay there totally relaxed, an idea occurred: *Instead of clapping while they type, why not beat their kundu drum? Yes! A familiar drum beat could possibly be helpful!*

Jim stayed with the diligent students for almost three hours. When he came home his face glowed. "Your students are ready for their next lesson," he informed me, visibly pleased. "The only problem I see is that they won't take their eyes off the typewriter. They're afraid they'll hit the wrong key."

The next morning, several stood outside the classroom waiting for me. "Why did you bring a drum?" Natalene wanted to know.

"You'll see," I promised. She took her seat, still looking puzzled. Two minutes later all 25 were in the room with paper in their machines and ready for class to begin.

"Okay, everyone! Place your hands on the home row!" I ordered, and took hold of the drum with my left hand. Are you ready to type the letters "f" and "j"? Remember to look at me, not down at the keyboard! Here we go!

"F-j space, f-j space," I repeated continually, pounding the drum with each syllable. The class caught on quickly and happily typed away. Their smiles lit the room.

Satisfied with their progress, I moved on to the letters "d"and "k". These proved a little harder for them, but they were determined. By noon they were able to type four letters with a space in-between. I tried not to notice their poor posture or the clumsy way their hands were poised on the home row. Beating the drum as they typed each letter helped them get the hang of it.

I didn't even think to ask for Your help, Lord, but You gave it to me anyway. Thank You, Jesus.

Again, the students practiced diligently all afternoon and would have stayed all night if Jim hadn't gone over and dismissed them. "Come back tomorrow," he told them, as he locked the door to keep them out.

Their enthusiasm never waned over the following six weeks. As I watched them copy paragraphs from books without looking at the keyboard, I felt sure they would all do well in their respective jobs. Not all were proficient, but the lights were definitely coming on.

On the last day of class, I had Cookie bake a cake. Although the students loved eating cake, they seemed more quiet than usual. I knew they were feeling sad about not having any more classes. In a way, I felt sad, too. In the days following, I missed the students more than I thought. At the same time, it felt luxurious to have so much extra time every morning to do my own typing. One day as I was typing a chapter from Psalms, Chululu came over and dropped an envelope on my desk.

"What's this?" I asked.

"Magunda sent us a package from Port Moresby. He put this letter inside the parcel for you."

Quickly, I slit the envelope open and pulled out a short note typed by my former student. It read:

"Dear Jaki, I am typing the way you taught me, but my friends in the office laugh at me. They say I type like a woman now. At first I felt ashamed, but now I know they wish they could type like me."

*Magunda used to type with two fingers, but
is now the envy of office friends.*

---

*"Count it all joy when you fall into various trials, knowing
that the testing of your faith produces patience." James 1:2–3
(NKJV)*

"Vea ka'ene ja venakia ani ani'ina piuni'avari vajijaho temarasa'avara. 'Ene ja nihejura. Joni nimairoiji vene kivujara reju'e
kisina rene hina va'ura." Jemisi 1:2–3

Chapter 22

Birth of the Bible School

Every Saturday morning Jim and I walked down to the lower end of the village where the market was located. There we bought fresh produce from the Managalasi people who lived in villages other than Numba.

The village market.

"It's almost 7:00," Jim reminded me. "Time to go!"

"I'm ready," I said, grabbing my stringbag. We hurried out the door, past the church and into the village. As we neared the market, we heard angry shouting.

"Who's that?" I asked Jim, not expecting an answer.

"Sounds like a fight," he replied. We picked up our pace. When we reached the market we saw two men physically fighting. Both men threw punches hard and fast, their faces contorted with hatred.

Many spectators gathered, but did nothing to stop the warfare. Chululu, too, stood unperturbed in the background near his wife, Pupudi who was unloading pineapples from her stringbag. She didn't seem concerned about the ruckus either. We walked in their direction.

"What's going on?" Jim asked Chululu, a little irritated that one of our village pastors should stand by and not try to settle the feud.

Chululu noted Jim's concern. "While you were at Ukarumpa these past months, other denominations have entered the plateau," he explained. "Their teachings are different than ours. These two men started arguing early this morning, each insisting that his denomination is the right one. Now it's come to this."

Chululu spoke in a normal tone of voice, as if the arguing and fighting were everyday occurrences. "Sometimes four or five from each village get involved, then the fighting gets out of hand," he explained further. "Twice I had to go get the police. It's better to stay out of the way until they arrive; only the police can make them stop."

"Oh, so that's why no one is trying to stop the fight," I exclaimed, looking at Jim for his reaction. "It would be too dangerous! That's a good reason to stand by and do nothing, isn't it?"

"Another thing," Chululu interjected. "People are not allowed to enter another village unless they hold the same doctrinal beliefs as those who live there do. If they don't, they have to go down the mountain and around and then back up again on the other side."

Jim and I stood stock still and looked at Chululu, our eyes wide with shock.

"This unofficial rule came to be while you were working at Ukarumpa," he added.

Jim appeared crestfallen, as if he might crumple. "Who started teaching the people to believe differently than what the Bible teaches?" he managed to choke out through a constricted throat.

Before Chululu could reply, I looked away. I wanted to hear more, but I'd heard enough and chose to hear the whole story later, in the privacy of our home. I left Jim with Chululu discussing the problem and walked over to Pupudi to buy a pineapple. Her face brightened. "This is the ripest one I have," she informed me, holding up one pineapple. "It will taste so sweet and juicy, you'll wish you bought two."

"Okay, give me another one," I said in mock resignation, and we laughed together. I was glad for our interaction as it gave me a brief distraction from the fighting and the hurt Jim was experiencing at the moment.

All of a sudden the assault on my senses was overwhelming. I wandered over to where Vavao's wife, Elizabeth, was selling baked goods. Her reputation as a superb baker had spread to all the villages. No doubt she would sell every scrap of bread within the hour. The fragrant aroma of the hot bread drew me to her stall.

Elizabeth uncovered the steaming bread, and I began placing the rolls I would buy on the counter in front of her. "Jaki, I'm so sorry I don't have a clean bag for you to put the rolls in," she said, looking concerned. Then she reached for a banana leaf to wrap the rolls in.

"Don't worry about that," I assured her, and the smile returned to her face. She placed the rolls in rows of three and carefully folded a banana leaf around each row, tucking the ends in and finally securing the bundles together with string.

"After all these years, I'm used to banana leaves," I informed her. "Sometimes Jim and I use banana leaves like dishes and eat off of them just like you." Happily, I accepted the parcel she handed me and stuffed it into my string bag along with the pineapples. Then, I signaled to Jim that I was ready to go.

As we slowly made our way out of the market, Donald, the policeman, arrived in a hurry and bolted over to where the action was taking place. He carried his club in one hand, poised and ready to use. The stern-looking policeman stepped into the fray and grabbed the shoulder of one of the brawlers, spinning him around so they faced each other. The fighting ceased immediately.

Exiting the market area, I asked Jim: "Did you see how fast those two men stopped fighting when Donald got there?"

Chululu heard me and said: "They know they would have to go to jail in Popondetta if they didn't stop fighting at once."

"At least they respect the law," I remarked to Jim when we reached the pathway that led back up into the village. Jim didn't respond. He was still troubled about the whole episode.

Chululu walked home with us, eager to help me translate my devotional. The tantalizing scent of the fresh bread I carried made our mouths water as we walked homeward. Chululu knew a cup of coffee and a warm roll with butter lay ahead. Since Pupudi didn't buy flour to bake bread, this would be a rare treat for him. The thought made me happy, too, but even more than our delightful snack, I anticipated working with this talented man. I always learned new things about the culture when Chululu and I discussed Scripture together. Likewise, my young teacher eagerly embraced new things from me that he could use when it was his turn to preach the sermon. I couldn't wait to get home so we could get started.

As we walked up the hill towards Numba, Chululu told us more disheartening news. "Some of the church leaders are running around with other men's wives," he said bluntly. "That's another reason why there's always strife and contention. Our churches are now like the Corinthian church. The problems they faced in Corinth are happening in our churches here."

The truth of Chululu's words deepened Jim's grief. Not knowing how to solve the problems made the days ahead look bleak.

As soon as we stepped into the house, I put water in the kettle and set it on the stove to boil. Next, I gingerly pulled out butter from the fridge for the warm rolls. Studying the Word with Chululu was all the medicine I needed, but Jim's hurt pierced deeper than mine. He picked up his Bible and disappeared into his study. I stirred him a cup of Milo and took it into the study with a buttered roll. Jim had already closed his eyes in prayer, so I quietly left the snack next to his Bible and went out wondering if he would ever lighten up again.

I prayed a short prayer for his peace of mind as I poured two cups of coffee. Setting the cups on a tray with the buttered rolls, I went to join Chululu at my desk.

Jim's burden deepened over the following months. Hope seemed a continent away. Day after day, Jim asked the Lord to show him a way to help the people out of their confusion. Knowing God's timing was perfect, he waited patiently for His answer.

One night he woke up suddenly with a prompting of God's Spirit telling him: *Bring all the groups from the different villages together and teach them what the Word of God says.* With that, the words "Bible Seminar" popped into his head.

Jim pushed back the covers and sat up in bed. He knew I was awake, so went on to tell me that he had a strong feeling about bringing the pastors, priests, and church leaders from all the villages together for a Bible seminar.

"I'll begin by teaching them how a person is saved. Some have graduated from denominational schools and know the dogma, liturgy and rituals, but they don't know how to lead another person to Christ."

"Uh-huh," I agreed sleepily, and pushed myself to pay attention to all he was saying.

"So that will be my starting point, and I'll go from there," he finished. Feeling elated that God had shown him a way to resolve the problem, he settled back onto his pillow, relaxed and soon fell asleep.

At dawn Chris was in the yard chopping wood. I heard Jim open the door and step outside onto the porch. "Chris," he called, "Go and tell Pastors Michael and Chululu to come to the house now."

"Okay," Chris replied, but first finished building the fire under the large blackened pot that he had already filled with water. Then he went off in the direction of Michael's house. Ten minutes later both Michael and Chululu walked into the kitchen looking curious. Jim and I were getting ready to eat breakfast. Before I sat down at the table, I quickly fixed the men a cup of hot Milo.

"Here, sit down," Jim offered, pulling out the chairs on either side of him. Then he proceeded to tell them his plan for teaching the church leaders. By the time Jim finished talking, Michael's jaw had dropped open. He tried to speak, but nothing escaped his mouth but warm air.

Finally, Chululu spoke, managing a feeble, "What?"

Jim pretended not to notice the shocked expressions. "We'll hold classes in the literacy house every morning; I'll teach them what the Bible says about believing in Christ *alone* for salvation."

As I carried the steaming cups of Milo to the table, I noted doubt expressed on their faces. "But," Jim went on, "we'll have to decide what dates would be best so the seminar won't interfere with garden work or coffee harvesting. You two will have to invite each leader individually," he told them bluntly. Then he sat back with his cup of Milo and waited for their response.

Michael spoke up first. "Most of those men won't come to our village; they know we don't believe their doctrines. They already told us not to walk through their villages," he said in an anxious tone. "If you want these church leaders to come to the Bible seminar, *you'll* have to be the one to invite them."

"Yes, that's the only way they'll come," Chululu agreed, substantiating Michael's argument. "They'll listen to you, but if Michael or I ask them, they won't come."

"Okay," Jim conceded. The frown on his face told us he wasn't happy with the decision. "Give me the names of every church leader in all the villages, and I'll write each one personally." Now Jim spoke softly to allay their anxieties. "I'll tell them that I'm not going to teach about denominations, but only teach what the Word of God says."

"Yes, if you tell them that, the leaders and teachers may come. But if they think you're going to tell them their denomination is wrong, they won't come," Michael advised.

"I understand," Jim assured them, "I'll tell them that I won't put their denomination down, nor will I start a new denomination. But both of you are going to have to make them feel welcome here. Forget about past disagreements! Let them know you're glad they came to study the Word of God."

"Yes, we'll do that," Chululu consented readily.

"*If* they come, we'll make them feel welcome," Michael repeated. Obviously, he had his doubts. Tipping his head back, he finished his Milo with one big gulp. "But don't count on their coming to our village," he warned. "There's too much anger right now."

"Well, you know what makes them angry, so don't talk about those things. Just talk about the Lord and the things you'll be learning in class," Jim suggested.

"Alright. Let us know when you have the invitations ready and we'll see that they get to the church leaders," Michael said slowly, almost reluctantly.

"Well," I interrupted, "if you'll give Jim the names now, I'll type the invitations today and give them to you this evening."

Jim retreated to his study for a pen and some lined paper. "Okay," he said, striding back to his chair. "Let's start with the pastors and leaders in Awaru Village."

I cleared the dishes from the table as Chris carried in

the hot water from outside where he had built the fire earlier. He glanced at me and returned my smile. In my heart, I felt that positive steps towards solving the problem were beginning to happen!

The first day for the seminar arrived. We had no idea how many men would come. Jim and I waited at the kitchen table, tapping our pencils and looking over our notes. Since the classes would take most of the day, Jim and I decided to take turns teaching. Jim would start, then I would take the third hour. In this way we could conserve our strength to prepare for the next day's lesson as well as help with homework assignments in the afternoons.

The clock struck twelve; only four leaders had arrived. I felt disappointed, but Jim had decided beforehand to teach the class even if only one man showed up.

Jim began teaching promptly at 1:00 p.m. It wasn't long before seven others wandered into the classroom looking uneasy. They searched for a place to sit at the back. Before the class ended, 12 students had arrived.

On the second day, still more church leaders showed up. As the day wore on, the students seemed to relax and appeared anxious to discuss the material presented. Word of the seminar spread, and by the third day, 40 men were present. They all seemed hungry to learn God's Word. And, as promised, Jim and I taught only from the Word of God.

Ezekiel prays for a way to receive Bible School training.

During lunch breaks, we noticed that as the students ate together, they discussed with each other the things they were learning. There were no signs of anger or disagreement. As they learned to love God's Word, they learned to love one another. By the end of the week, all the men had become good friends. After the second week, when the seminar ended, the students wanted to continue studying.

"Can you make the sessions longer?" one pastor asked. "Maybe three weeks?"

"We want to keep on learning," Ezekiel, a church leader, stated on behalf of the others, "but we don't have money to go to Bible School in Port Moresby. Can we just continue coming here to study the Bible?"

I sensed that God had done something powerful during the two weeks for these students. And so, from the hearts' desire of these men, the Ese Bible Institute was born.

"For I know the plans I have for you," declares the Lord, "plans to prosper you and not to harm you, plans to give you hope and a future." Jeremiah 29:11 (NIV)

"Ara tuna'i hia ka'ene hihunijaho nihena kamarejo amair-iaravuta. Oni amairiara ka'ene Nara amairiaravujaho a'e sise'i ahahuna pana kaivo na maranahuna'e amairiaravuta. Amairiara ka'ene vea tuna'i hihunijine 'ee oni nimaaro ka'ene a ijihuni toi nimai roji'i hihunijaho Nara vajahuna." Jeramaia 29:11

Chapter 23

God Settles A Dispute

The next day, over lunch, Jim and I talked about the problems that would arise from going ahead with a Bible School. "I don't think the two of us could handle it alone," I proposed. "We're going to need help, like more teachers to share the teaching load. And some builders! We should build a brand-new building to use solely for the Bible school. What do you think?"

"Building the school won't be a problem," Jim replied quickly. "There's plenty of guys in the village who would jump at the chance to help build. Everybody wants to earn money so they can buy tinned meat or fish, or rice, and on it goes. And most families still need money to pay their kids' school fees for next year, so there won't be any problem getting helpers to build a school building.

"To me," Jim continued thoughtfully, "the biggest problem is land. I don't know where we would build the school. No one in the village has any land to spare, and …"

Before Jim could finish, a frantic knock came at the door. "Jim! Jim!" a familiar voice yelled out. Both of us knew instantly it was Pastor Michael.

"Something's up," Jim remarked as he shoved back from the table.

"Oh, oh," I replied as Jim strode to the front door and

pulled it open. Michael immediately began blurting out the reason for the urgency of his coming.

"It's George Mauwi!" he gushed. "He went to the airstrip this morning with his sons and removed all the cones from the landing strip!"

"Oh, no!" I said to myself. *That means no planes will be allowed to fly in and land.*

"What? Why would he do a thing like that?" Jim asked, lines of concern forming around his eyes.

"Because the airstrip was Mauwi's ground in the first place," Michael went on to explain. "The government bought it from him so that planes could fly in and take our coffee to Popondetta, otherwise we would have no way of selling our coffee."

"Did Mauwi receive payment for the land?"

"Yes!"

"Then that finalized it!" Jim said adamantly. "The man has no right to take away the cones."

Michael explained further: "Mauwi wants more money, so he is reclaiming his land. His sons, too, say they weren't paid enough for the ground.

"All the villages are talking about what they did. Everyone knows that no planes can fly in and land without the cones. That's why everybody is angry at George Mauwi and his family. Now we'll have to hire large trucks to drive our coffee to Popondetta, but nobody has money to hire trucks."

Michael looked hopelessly at Jim. Jim looked back at the disheartened pastor and held eye contact with him to be sure he would get the message: "Listen! The reason the government put the strip there," Jim began, "was to help you people move your coffee to Popondetta to sell. Without the cones there to mark the landing boundaries, it won't be possible. Mauwi and his family could get into a lot of trouble for doing what they did."

Later that afternoon, several men and a few women from other villages started congregating on our front porch to get ready for a meeting. They muttered about George Mauwi taking the cones away and causing problems for everybody.

When several more men arrived, they decided to go up into the village and meet in the large empty building known as *the wind house*. There were no walls on this building, just a floor built up off the ground with a roof over the top. People often met there to eat food and fellowship together.

Since everyone insisted that Jim come, Jim was persuaded to attend the meeting. They knew how important it was to have our SIL planes land on the airstrip with our supplies or with visitors. Jim consented to attend and, just before leaving the house, took a minute to look for the letter in his file from the government. It stated that Mauwi no longer owned the land, but it was now officially government-owned.

Once everyone was settled in the wind house, the talk turned to Mauwi collecting big money from the government every month. Even though the man no longer owned the land, he had collected almost 20,000 kina. The government provided Mauwi with this money for the express purpose of maintaining the airstrip, but the former land owner had not done a speck of maintenance, he just pocketed the money.

In order for aircraft to fly in and land safely, the airstrip had to be maintained and the grass cut short. Therefore,

Jim and Pastor Michael chose six men to go to Sila and cut the grass regularly. Jim paid these men to do Mauwi's job.

The meeting was about to begin. Fifty or more men plus a few women crammed under the shelter and sat closely together on the bamboo-woven floor. Then, at the last minute, Mauwi and two of his sons showed up, surprising everyone. The few women stood promptly, looking embarrassed, and scrambled off the platform to make room for the men. The three late-comers squeezed in at the end of the over-crowded wind house and sat with their legs folded beneath them. Everyone then looked to Jim and waited for him to speak.

Jim leaned back against a large post that held up a part of the roof. The house grew silent, waiting expectantly. Michael sat down next to Jim. In a low tone, Jim requested Michael to conduct the meeting on his behalf and to begin by greeting everybody.

The pastor cleared his throat loudly and welcomed everyone to Numba Village. Without wasting a second, he broached the subject: "We're here to talk about the problem of not being able to fly our coffee to Popondetta because the cones have been removed from the airstrip."

"That's right!" one of the men from Kweno Village spat out. Heads nodded around the floor suggesting that this was definitely serious business. The Kweno man stared hard at Mauwi and asked: "Why did you take the cones away?"

Mauwi unashamedly stared back at the man. "The government hasn't paid me enough money for my land, and I want it back," he replied firmly. His voice held angry tones. "I need the land to make more gardens so my family won't be hungry."

Both sons agreed heartily, insisting that their father get paid more money or that the land be given back to him.

"Well, you have to fly to Port Moresby," Michael repeated after Jim advised him. "Go to the Government house and talk to *them* about it. Let them know about the land and money problems you are having."

"I don't have money to buy a ticket to fly to Port Moresby," Mauwi complained.

Everyone present knew the man was lying, but no one challenged him because he was older than anyone else present. In the Managalasi culture it was unacceptable to accuse an older person of lying. No one spoke, and the room became uncomfortably silent.

Jim felt that now was the time he, himself, should speak. He leaned over and reached into his back pocket to get the letter he brought with him. All eyes focused on him as he unfolded the paper and began to read its contents. When he finished, he went through the letter again, rewording the contents in simple terms so all present could understand.

Jim then looked into Mauwi's eyes wanting his full attention. "This letter states that you no longer own the land," he told him, deliberately elongating each word. "It now belongs to the government, and you and your sons had no right to go and remove the cones that they put there."

"Yes, that's right, that's right!" several men said at once.

"You must return all the cones to where they were!" another said, and all agreed. Their voices grew louder and louder.

It was clear to see that Mauwi and both sons were getting angry. Mauwi stood up in the crowded room and raised his fist. "My sons and I are going to the airstrip right now!" he declared to everyone. "We're going to take our shovels and dig a trench across the airstrip! Then we'll make a big fire and destroy all the cones!"

With that, he jumped from the house to the ground, followed by his sons. The three men started for their village, ranting and raving as they went. Everyone else remained in the wind house, sitting quietly and looking defeated. Slowly, the men began to discuss the problems that would no doubt arise from an airstrip with a trench dug across the middle. Finally they asked Jim what to do.

Jim didn't see any way out of the sticky mess. He saw fear and anger on their faces, yet he felt he had said all he could say and folded the government letter back into his pocket. He hoped his action would signal to all that the meeting had come to an end. Instead, the prompt departure of Mauwi and sons started an angry process that could go long into the night.

The men began peppering Jim with questions in a staccato style without expressing much emotion. They kept their voices level trying to substitute intensity for what was their rawest emotion — anger.

After an hour of talk, the weather grew misty. When the mist turned to rain, the men from other villages grabbed their belongings and started hastily for their villages. Jim, too, with shoulders hunched, headed home quickly in the rain. He entered the house, a portrait of gloom.

"Got any hot water?" he asked. "I'm ready for a hot drink; either tea or Milo will do."

"What happened at the meeting to get you so upset?" I asked, concerned.

"I'm just getting too old to handle these kinds of problems, he admitted, and reached for a towel to dry himself off.

I made Jim a steaming cup of Milo and myself some decaf. As we sat at the table drinking, the rain started coming down harder. We decided not to start the generator, but to just make a fire in the fireplace and relax quietly before going to bed.

That night, the rain pelted down harder. Seemingly end-less bolts of lightning lit up the sky as rolling thunder crashed throughout the night. *Will it ever end?* I wondered.

I woke up just as the morning's first hint of light started peeking through. The rain had finally stopped. I noticed Jim sitting on the edge of the bed. "What's wrong?" I asked.

"My back feels stiff, and my head congested. I must have sat too long on that hard floor yesterday."

My eyebrows arched. "Would a massage help?" I offered. Before he could answer, we heard voices outside. The voices grew louder as they got closer. When their footsteps reached our porch, the voices quieted down.

"Jimmy-o!" someone called out strongly.

"Oi!" Jim replied in Managalasi fashion. "I'm coming!"

Hurriedly, we both went down the hall to see what brought these visitors at such an early hour. Michael stood outside with Chris, Chululu, and a few other villagers. Chululu spoke up as soon as Jim opened the door: "Jim!" he addressed in an urgent tone of voice. "Late last night a bolt of lightning hit Mauwi's house and struck it down. No one else's house was hit, only Mauwi's."

Chris, his eyes intently on Jim, spoke up: "After the meet-ing yesterday, Mauwi and his sons left our village and went to Sila Airstrip. They took shovels and dug a trench across the field so that no planes could land there anymore."

"After the bolt of lightning hit his house last night," Chululu broke in, "his sons ran to see if their parents died.

Nobody in the house was hurt, but the house is ruined. It fell down completely."

"Mauwi and his sons were terrified," Michael put in, "so the men gathered up the cones that they stored under their houses and carried them all back up to the airstrip. And the trench they dug is now refilled," Chris added, nodding his head up and down.

Our messengers appeared calm and in control, but Jim and I knew they were in a highly emotional state. Jim opened his mouth to say what was already obvious, but couldn't speak. The flu bug had gotten to him. He tried again in a hoarse whisper, but his voice was completely gone.

The men stared back at him expectantly, but no one said a word.

No words were necessary.

"Do not merely look out for your own personal interests, but also for the interests of others." Philippians 2:4 (NASB)

"Ene joni ura ijiru pa'ajo'avara kaivo ea ahopuni ura ijija u'o ki'avara." Piripai 2:4

Chapter 24

A Cry to God

Someone was blowing the conch shell for the second time — time for church. "Get a move on!" Jim called to me from the kitchen. Then, "I'm going!" and went on without me.

In the Managalasi culture men and women never sat together, so I waited at home, listening for the singing to begin. Wasting time, I snuggled the cat and played with the dog for a few minutes. Then, after two hymns were sung, I strolled across the grassy field to church.

During the greeting song, Chululu was the first to come over and shake my hand. Happiness swept through me, as Chululu had been very ill the past week. But his name was on the calendar to preach today. Apparently, he didn't bother to find a substitute. In his sermon he talked about *believing* in Christ to save us, not doing a lot of good works. During his message, the Gospel was clearly presented.

Ahusa, a younger woman, sat on the log next to me. She was using the old translated version of the New Testament. Still, I was happy to see she could find all the passages when Chululu announced them. I showed her my newly revised Bible and compared how the verses differed. "You should buy a *new* Bible," I encouraged. "They only cost two kina."

"I want one, but I don't have any money," she replied, and looked down at her feet, as though ashamed.

"Bring me a white yam and a papaya tomorrow, and I'll give you two kina," I promised.

Ahusa looked up at me hopefully, but said nothing. I couldn't be certain whether she thought that was a good idea or not.

The following afternoon as I was preparing dinner, Ahusa came to the house with a white yam, a papaya and some ears of corn.

"I'm so glad you came to buy the newer version of God's Word!" I told her with a smile.

"I've been praying for a copy," she said. "I told God I had no money and to please provide a way for me to have my own Book. I cried out to Him, but I didn't know if He heard me or not. Then last Sunday you sat down next to me in Church and told me I could earn a copy by bringing a white yam. I want to tell you 'thank you,' but I know it was God who provided my Bible, so I'm going to tell Him 'thank you' instead."

I couldn't trust myself to speak, so moved was I by her words. Quickly, I disappeared into the study and returned holding up a New Testament. I handed her the Book, and her face lit up.

"Ese, Jaki," she said and turned to leave. Then she turned back toward me again and grasped my hand, holding on to it tightly. I opened my mouth to tell her how happy she made me and to also thank her for the food, but I couldn't get the lump out of my throat.

Ahusa, as if sensing my emotional struggle, promptly let loose her grasp and scampered out the front door.

I stood at the doorway and watched her go, then went back inside to sit at the table and talk to God:

Thank You, Lord, for the opportunity to sit next to Ahusa last Sunday, and for making me the channel through which her prayer was answered.

"So then, while we have opportunity, let us do good to all men, and especially to those who are of the household of the faith." Galatians 6:10 (NASB)

"Enakune nu vea mamaa ape'avajaho roe nu ea maho'o puna'i hami ve'avara vo maraku'a ea ka'ene nimaa roji'ini jihipuna'i hami ve'avara." Karesia 6:10

Chapter 25

The Hungriest People

As usual, the mailbag arrived on the next plane. I pawed through a stack of letters and spotted one from Tanya. Tearing into it, I read, "I met someone who wants to go to Papua New Guinea. He's a great Bible teacher, Dad, and believes the same way you believe, so you won't have to worry about false doctrines.

"A Mr. Gene Cunningham was our guest speaker at church last Sunday. After the service, I introduced myself to him and his wife, Nan. He told me he would like to go to Papua New Guinea, but needed an invitation from someone who worked there. I told him about you and the work you are doing. I think he'll be getting in touch with you soon."

He did.

Just three months after Tanya's letter introduced them, Gene and Nan Cunningham arrived. As soon as we met, I knew they were made out of the right stuff, especially after hearing the story of their arrival from Popondetta to our village.

215

"We had quite a journey coming here in a four-wheel drive," Gene began. "We bogged down about six times. And when we got to any bridges we had to put planks in front of the truck in order to drive across.

"When we got to Afore, the government station, the driver told us we couldn't go any further, so we spent the night there. When we woke up the next morning we noted that there was nothing but clouds between the station and here. The people there told us, 'That's where you're going—up above those clouds.' It looked pretty exciting to us and we took off walking.

Arrival of Gene and Nan to Numba Village.

"It rained on us pretty much the whole day. We slipped and fell in the mud and arrived looking like two drowned rats. As we came walking into the village, all the men started cheering. Jim was teaching the men in the church building. I had never met him before, and we met for the first time through the window of the church where we shook hands.

"'Go on to the house,' he told us. 'Jaki has some things ready for you.' So we met Jaki at the house and got dried out. Then, after a hearty meal, Nan and I got caught up on what was happening in Numba Village."

The next morning Gene taught the men's seminar while Nan held children's meetings. Happy kids crammed into the room eager to hear Bible stories and then work on a craft project which Nan brought with her from the States.

Children happily display their crafts.

When the week had ended, Gene informed us over supper, "I've been all over the world teaching students the Bible: India, Africa, South America and Australia. But I have never seen men so hungry for the Word of God as right here in your village."

My eyes widened in shock. Jim raised his head and we exchanged glances.

Gene noted my look of astonishment and asked, "Does this surprise you, Jaki?"

"No, it doesn't surprise me, Gene, it blows me away!"

Gene's curiosity was piqued, and he waited for further explanation.

"When Jim and I first arrived," I went on, my dry eyes filling at the memory, "these very people told us they didn't want our God. 'Go back to America!' they said. 'We don't want your American god, we have our own gods!'

"And they did — they worshipped the spirits of their dead ancestors. They prayed to these spirits when they got sick, when they planted new gardens, when they went hunting for meat and when they performed their traditional dances."

"Why would they pray to ancestor spirits when they danced?" Gene inquired.

"The people danced when they finished planting their gardens to celebrate the end of their hard labor. Then they asked the spirits to bless their gardens and give them a lot of food so they wouldn't be hungry during the upcoming year."

Again, Gene looked at me inquisitively. "What made them think the spirits would hear them and give an abundance of food?"

Jim broke in: "The older people taught them that philosophy. Whatever happens, good or bad, is because of the spirits," he explained.

"Another thing," I added. "There's a certain kind of

"magical" flower the people planted in their gardens. These, too, were somehow connected with spirits to produce bountiful gardens.

"So, you see, your comment made me realize anew all that God has accomplished here — that people who once didn't want God, are now the hungriest people in the world for His Word!"

I was fighting with every fiber of my being not to break down and start blubbering. "It's miraculous!" I managed to choke out.

Gene looked back and forth from Jim to me. "Well, if you're serious about building a Bible School, I'm training some Bible teachers in Perth, Australia, right now. If you get students and classes lined up, I'll see that teachers and a two-year curriculum are provided. After two years each student will receive a diploma."

"That sounds great!" Jim acknowledged, "but it looks like we're going to need another miracle."

"And what's that?" Gene asked, both eyebrows raised.

"Well, we need to build a school, but there's a problem — land. The village people don't have enough land to plant their gardens let alone give it away for a school building. I've been talking to some men about the need, but none want to give up their land. They need it too badly to provide food for their families."

"That's understandable," Gene said quickly. "We'll have to make that a matter of prayer."

"There is one man who is willing to give his land for the school," Jim added. "You know him, Gene, it's Aparihi, the man who interprets for you. You may know him as Pastor Michael."

"Oh, sure, I know who he is."

"Well, he owns some land close to the church building.

Aparihi, the man who offered his land to build the
Ese Bible Institute.

A few weeks ago we went to look at it; the spot would be perfect for the school! In fact, Aparihi and his two brothers got so excited, they got their machetes and began clearing the land. That's when they came across the problem — two coconut trees need to be cut down. But the trees don't belong to Aparihi or his family, they belong to another man."

"Would it be possible to buy them?" Gene inquired.

"Well, when we built the church, we had to cut down several coconut trees," Jim explained. "We paid 100 kina for each tree, and the owners were happy. We offered the same amount for these two trees, but the owner said he wanted 200 kina for each tree and wouldn't budge from that price. Aparihi said 200 kina was too much for one tree and refused the man's offer. So we left."

"That's too bad," Gene commented before going on. "God tells us to leave our burdens at His feet, and He also tells us to ask, and it will be given. Let's do that and just wait and see what God does about the problem.

"And all things you ask in prayer, believing, you shall receive."
Matthew 21:22 (NASB)

"'Ene ja niho'o nimaa nimai ro'i kaivo unenu'u 'aho'a Godi jari'avajaho ja 'ekahuna 'iamana." Matiu 21:22

Chapter 26

An Unexpected Request

Marija, my village father, coughed incessantly every day. He could no longer tolerate the medicine I gave him, and helplessly, I watched him growing weaker.

Even though I knew he was dying, I felt shock when I heard someone call to me from outside the kitchen window: "Jaki! Your father died!"

Something like dread passed through my body, but it went deeper than that. This elderly man whom I called *Amo* had been caring for me since we first arrived in 1962. How would I continue life in the village without his love and support?

Thoughts of his visits seemed to flood my mind. I recalled the day when he sat on our couch and looked at me accusingly: "Why didn't you come and tell my mother and father how to go to heaven before it was too late for them?" he reproached.

Why that scene specifically came to mind, I don't know. Perhaps to remind me that Amo was now in heaven with the Lord he so strongly believed in.

Someone knocked at the front door. I went around quickly and found Mainare standing in the doorway, her face distorted, her eyes watery.

"Oh, Mainare, I'm so sorry about your father," I said as my arms went around her.

"Jaki, I want you to say something at my father's funeral," she stated matter of factly. Then she gently pushed my arms away and took a step backwards, emphasizing the gravity of her request.

"What?" I asked unnecessarily. I had heard what she said, but didn't want to believe what she was asking.

"We'll hold the funeral service tomorrow in front of my house," she continued, ignoring my question. "You're his daughter, too! Joshua, Jon Mari and I want you to speak at the service."

Unprepared for this request, I hemmed and hawed before replying. "Shouldn't a man speak?"

"No!" she replied quickly. "Amo would want you to speak! You're his *daughter! You're family!*"

Her insistence stunned me. I thought about Gene possibly being present for the funeral and having to listen to a woman speak. I felt intimidated, wondering how to respond. There was a long silence.

Mainare saw the fear on my face and touched my arm. "Everybody is at my house waiting. What should I tell them?

"Yes," I said finally. "He's my father, and I will speak!"

Relief swept over her face. "Okay," she replied, and started for the door.

After she left, I quickly headed for the bedroom. The shock of speaking at my village father's funeral overpowered me. I picked up my Bible from the side table by the bed and jotted down some thoughts about eternal life from John's Gospel.

The night was short, I couldn't sleep, even had I wanted to. My head throbbed as I reached for my funeral notes in the early morning light.

"Got your sermon ready?" Jim deadpanned. I looked over at him and noted the mischief in his eyes.

"That's not funny!" I bristled.

"Oh, you'll do fine," he soothed. "Just tell them what heaven is like, that Marija won't be coughing or having pain anymore. It'll be good for the family to think about that."

"I will," I agreed. Then, changing the subject: "Jim, would you oversee breakfast this morning? I want to go over my notes."

"Yeah," he replied. "Jupo's making toast and the water is getting hot. I think Gene is ready for coffee."

At 10 o'clock Jon Mari came to the house. "Jaki!" he called from the front porch. "We're ready to begin. Can you come now?"

"Yes! I'm coming!" I called back. Then I turned to Jupo. "Joop, go to the school and tell Jim that the service is starting now."

"Alright," she said, and rushed out the back door.

Jon Mari waited for me on the porch. I honestly didn't know what to expect as we walked together to Mainare's house. I tried to breathe normally, but it was becoming next to impossible.

"Is everyone there?" I asked lamely, cutting into the silence.

"Yes, we're all ready."

In no time we were approaching Mainare's house. My legs

were rubbery and my stomach rolled when I saw Amo lying at the foot of the stairway wrapped up tightly from neck to feet in a pandanus mat. Then my eyes popped open when I saw that he was wearing Jim's baseball cap. As though Jon Mari read my mind, he said: "Amo told us that when he died, he wanted to be buried wearing the hat Jim gave him."

The group of about 50 who had gathered at Mainare's house began to sing a hymn. I studied my father's form elevated on a platform made with sawn wood. Amo wore a normal expression and appeared to be resting comfortably. Several people stood on the porch leaning over the railing as they sang. Others sat on the steps and on the ground across the pathway.

As soon as the hymn ended, a panic began to feast on me. I looked at Joshua who nodded for me to speak. I swallowed a deep breath and pushed the air down into my lungs, past my heart, which was beating loudly. Without wasting time, I moved next to the body and began by telling the story of the first day I met Amo.

"He was carrying his shotgun," I said, "and, not understanding why Jim and I had come, threatened to shoot us if we tried to steal the land."

As I went on telling stories of how I became his daughter, I felt the tension leave my body. The interest shown on the faces of the spectators egged me on, and, to my surprise, I found I was actually enjoying the interaction.

As I was speaking, Jim arrived with Gene and the entire classroom of students. Without commenting on their arrival, I went on to explain that Amo really wasn't here wrapped in a mat, that his body was just the "house" he lived in while here on earth. But now he is with God and won't have any more sickness. But *we* will have pain and sickness until we go to be with God," I explained to the group.

Finally, I opened my Managalasi New Testament and read Philippians 1:21: "For to me, to live is Christ and to die is gain."

Everybody seemed happy with those assuring words, and I nodded to Joshua, signaling that I was finished.

"Thank you, Jaki. You were a good daughter to our father." Then he turned toward the Bible School instructor. "Gene, would you like to say something?"

Not looking at all surprised, Gene nodded his head, indicating that he would. "I'll need an interpreter," he reminded us.

Chululu, who happened to be standing right next to him, agreed to interpret.

Gene then began to tell all of us what a believer will see after he dies. "What did Marija see as he stepped through death's door and on home to Christ?"

Amo's body was wrapped securely in pandanus mats before burial.

Gene painted word pictures about Marija arriving in the city of God. After he finished, Joshua thanked him and nodded to some of the men sitting on the ground in front of the porch. They stood quickly and positioned themselves around the body. Then, in unison they lifted the platform and were ready to carry Amo's body to the cemetery for burial. First, they stood by and waited patiently while Mainare wrapped a new towel around her father's head. Gene and the students headed back to the school. Jim and I walked along trailing behind them. I wondered forlornly who would fill the huge gap Amo was leaving behind. As we strolled towards the school building, I overheard one of the students remark: "My feet were here on the ground, but I just took a trip to heaven and back."

Suddenly, I felt myself smiling. Did most of the people at the funeral feel the same way? With all my heart I hoped so. And this student expressed it perfectly.

"After that, we who are still alive and are left will be caught up together with them in the clouds to meet the Lord in the air. And so we will be with the Lord forever." 1 Thessalonians 4:17 (NIV)

"'Ejakame nu ea ka'ene mai'o hi'avajija 'urina va'e kahi 'imitia vaji pu piunime ahuma ajima va'e ichutoi Natohwijaho piunahuna." 1 Tesaronia 4:17

Chapter 27

God's Intervention

Through the classes, many men saw that the things they were teaching in their villages were not in the Bible.

During the second week of the seminar, Jim and I sat in the back of the class as Gene taught, and learned along with the men. Jim's aim for the class was to help the pastors see that some of the doctrines they were teaching in their churches were not in the Bible. Gene had done a masterful job of showing them these errors.

After the course ended, one pastor said, "Through these classes I've seen that I've been misleading my congregation. I must go back and apologize to them and tell them the truth from God's Word."

The second week had passed by all too quickly. Gene and Nan were packed and on their way to Sila Air Strip, the first leg of their journey back to the States. They both loved hiking, and walked up and down the mountains to Sila without needing to stop and rest. I sat in back of Jim on the motorbike and enjoyed riding to the airstrip. Many students tagged along to bid their beloved teacher farewell.

The plane landed soon after Jim and I arrived. Gene and Nan were already there waiting. "They're all going to miss you," I said to Gene on behalf of the students.

"Well, we'll go back to our church and tell our people about the need. We'll do everything we can to get a Bible School started here."

Waving goodbye to Nan and Gene at Sila Airstrip.

We all watched forlornly as Nan and Gene climbed into the Cessna. Soon the engine revved up and the aircraft taxied to the top of the airstrip. The crowd of us waved hardily as they zoomed by and were airborne in seconds.

They're gone! I thought sadly, and began to focus on the hope Gene left with me — that a Bible School will possibly be established in these isolated mountains. Thrilled to the core, I couldn't wait to share this dream-come-true with our supporters. With their prayers, I felt assured it would happen a lot sooner.

Three weeks after the Cunninghams left, the weather made an unanticipated shift. A dense fog rolled in one morning, settling over the mountains. By 8:00 o'clock a howling storm pounded the village roofs, flooding the grounds around the houses, the church and the gardens. Lightning lit the skies as deafening thunder exploded.

And that's when it happened — during the thick of the storm, lightening severed both coconut trees — the ones that were keeping the Bible School from being built. Miraculously, no other trees were harmed, only the two belonging to the man who refused to sell them to Pastor Michael for 100 kina.

The message was clear: God had intervened and performed another miracle!

The destruction of the coconut trees became big news and sizzled through every village along the plateau. Everyone who had eyes to see and ears to hear knew without a doubt that the Ese Bible Institute was in God's plan for Numba Village.

"Consider it pure joy, my brothers, when you encounter various trials, knowing that the testing of our faith produces endurance." James 1:2–3 (NASB)

"'Ene vwehu nune hami vwihanc nirlsa'avara. Vea ka'ene ja venakia ani ani'ina piuni'avari vajijaho temarasa'avara. 'Ene joni nimairoji vene kivujara reju'e kisina rene hina va'ura."
Jemisi 1:2–3

Chapter 28

A Humbling
Expression of Love

Where had the years disappeared to? Another five had zoomed by, and it was time to leave the village again. For how long? Perhaps for good this time. Only God knew.

Cookie in the kitchen

As usual, a farewell party was planned. As I sat at the table writing a note, I could hear village friends beginning to gather outside. Instead of the party being held in the village as usual, it would be happening right outside our house in the grassy area between the Church and the helicopter pad.

Cookie just finished washing down the kitchen cupboards with antiseptic, setting the dishes upside down so the rats couldn't get to them while the house stood empty. All of a sudden, we heard a clatter on the porch. Someone was banging a metal object against the outside wall, making a racket. I lay aside the note I was writing and leaned over the table to get a good glimpse of who would be coming in the front door. Chululu walked in first with Chris following. Chris, carrying a large metal basin, gave it one last bang on the door before entering the house.

"Chris, why are you making so much noise?" I asked, arching my brows.

"For no reason," he replied nonchalantly. "I just felt like making noise." He handed the large metal basin to Cookie. She showed no surprise in her expression, almost like she was expecting the intrusion.

Both Chris and Chululu had towels draped over their shoulders, but it was too late to go down to the river and wash. Something was up.

Cookie took the basin and filled it with water.

The banging noise brought Jim in from his study. "What's going on?"

"We came to wash your feet, so both of you go and sit down," Chululu directed, pointing to the corner of the dining room where I was sitting with the pen still poised in my hand. Chululu waited for me to get up, then pushed the table out of the way to make room for the pan of water. Chris carried two chairs over and placed them facing each other.

"Who told you to wash our feet?" I asked incredulously, looking first to Chululu, then Chris. Both knew about Jesus washing His disciples' feet, but why would they wash ours?

"You're leaving us tomorrow," Chris explained, "and we have nothing worthy to give you for all you've done to help us, so we want to wash your feet."

"Sit down," Chululu said kindly, indicating the chairs Chris had arranged. "Put both feet into the basin."

Cookie joined us, carrying a kettle of warm water. Next, she pulled out three small bars of soap from her pocket and handed one to Chululu and one to Chris. The three kneeled down simultaneously and began washing our feet, ankles and lower legs.

Overwhelmed, I watched as they worked this act of love in silence. Cookie and Chululu, their faces serious, wiped tears away on their sleeves as they gently lathered Jim's feet. My husband sat with his eyes closed looking peaceful, yet humbled.

Five minutes later, they rubbed our feet dry with their towels. I felt I had just experienced an honor I never earned.

After they'd completed the beautiful ritual, the three of them stood up and laid the damp towels over their shoulders. I stood along with them. I was so moved I couldn't speak. All of us wept audibly as we embraced. Jim's long arms easily drew us close, and the five of us cried together shamelessly.

"I will never forget what you have done tonight," I blubbered.

"We will never forget you," Chris said.

"Well, you never know … we may be back," Jim said, ending the emotional evening on a more positive note.

"Yes!" they cried out in unison. "Come back!" For the first time tonight I saw hope in their expressions.

Chris bent over to pick up the basin of water and carried it to the sink. "Nobody wants you to leave, so if you tell everybody at the party tonight that you're coming back, we'll all be happy," he said, and poured the water into the sink.

Jim and Chululu put the table and chairs back into place. Then we heard the conch shell sounding: It was time for the farewell party to begin!

"Beloved, if God so loved us, we also ought to love one another."
1John 4:11 (NASB)

"Ehu nuna ka'ene na ja oja mihukije Godi Hu niho'o natohwa oja muha jihuna'e nu 'u'o ea 'aho pu'umo oja 'ekarahuna."
1 Joni 4:11

Chapter 29

The Farewell Party

Most of the Numba people had gathered food from their gardens yesterday and cooked it this morning. Some of the men had cut large banana leaves and arranged them in the area between our house and the Church for people to sit on.

A farewell party was planned.

Many were still coming with plates of hot yams, sweet potatoes, taros and roasted bamboo shoots as we arrived. Others were already sitting on the banana leaves waiting patiently.

My eyes flickered over our many friends who had gathered together, and the finality of our leaving penetrated deep down to my soul. *Would I ever live among them again?* A rush of grief swept over me. Quickly, I looked for a place to sit down before I fell down.

"Jaki! Come and sit over here!" Poki called. I looked up to see him pointing to a spot just in front of where he stood. A special new mat was placed in front of the log that had been rolled to where the activity would take place. Pupudi helped me down onto the mat and sat down beside me.

"Thank you, Pupudi," I said, and she smiled back at me. The night air felt chilly, and I quickly buttoned up my sweater. Reflections of the foot-washing lingered in my mind. I felt emotionally overwrought, and sat stiff as a board. Jim sauntered through the crowd, clearly enjoying himself as he chatted nonchalantly.

Poki, master of ceremonies at our farewell party, tells how God's Word came into existence in the Managalasi language.

Joshua and Jon Mari had carried out the pulpit from the

church and set it in front of the log where Poki stood. Luke, his son, fiddled beside him with some microphones intended for use during the evening. Poki now reached for a mic and put it to his mouth: "Okay, everyone, sit down and we'll ask God's blessing on the food," he announced. "Then Jim and Jaki will go first in line and get their food."

After the blessing, I got up and Pupudi handed me a plate. Bamboo shoots were my favorite, and I took two. "How long will it be before I eat these again?" I asked Jim who followed behind me filling his plate.

"I don't know, so you better eat up while you can," he replied in a serious tone.

While we ate, several stood to give short speeches, mainly to thank us for giving them God's Word in their language and for teaching them to read and write. Then, Turive, one of the older men, stood. "After you leave us tomorrow, what will we do when we get sick and need medicine?" he asked, keeping his eyes focused on Jim and me. "Many of us will die," he added without hope and sat down.

Others agreed under their breath and a desolate spirit began to spread over the group. Noting this, I spoke up from where I sat: "If you're not lazy and go down to the Medical Station at Sakarina, you will get the treatment you need." I was practically yelling so they would all hear. "If you can't walk well, ask your relatives to help you; otherwise, *yes!* You will die! So don't be lazy!"

After my sobering words, things quieted down. Then, unexpectedly, Anumari, one of the oldest women living in Numba, stood and calmly walked to the center where everyone could see her and hear what she was going to say. I was unprepared for her words:

"When you first came to our village, the ground was hard," she said, her eyes directed towards Jim and me. The atmosphere grew silent. "No one listened to your talk about God Finally, a seed pierced the ground and went down inside. After a while, a little sprout shot up, but it stayed little for a long time."

The old woman looked down and paused, as if trying to remember. No one moved or made a sound. After a few seconds, she looked up again and continued. "Then the rain came and watered the ground. Now the sprout has grown so big, it covers all the Managalasi land." Anumari returned quietly to her spot on the banana leaf and sat down.

My mouth went dry. I leaned over to Jim: "It was like she was speaking a parable to us," I whispered hoarsely.

"Yes! I've never heard anyone talk like that before," he replied. "And she said it so casually."

I looked around at the hundreds of others who continued to sit silently with stunned expressions. They knew, and we knew, that this elderly, uneducated woman who couldn't speak a word of English had, in a profound way, summed up what the village was like before our coming to what it is today.

Poki took advantage of the silence and got up. He walked to the pulpit and picked up the microphone. Looking slowly over those who had gathered, he announced: "Let's all bow in prayer and give God all the glory for what He has done for us."

"Lord, thank You for not allowing the ground in our village to remain hardened," he began, "but You watered the seed so it would sink in. Now we know the Truth and will live with you forever ...."

"Other seed fell on good soil. It came up, grew and produced a crop, multiplying thirty, sixty, or even a hundred times." Mark 4:8 (NIV)

"'Enakaivo 'ina 'aho'a mwe'a maa arihajaho riama marasahe 'ina aho'a mapoka rejume 'aho'a mapoka mapoka rejume 'aho'a niho'o mapoka mapoka rejara." Maka 4:8

Chapter 30

A Day of Rejoicing

Word of our returning to Numba after our trip to America got around the village, exciting everyone. Our farewell party, with Poki as an enthusiastic master of ceremonies, was upbeat. There was plenty of laughing and Poki did a remarkable job of conducting the program and introducing each speaker.

Focusing my mind on Poki, I knew it was God who gave us this special person in the year 1962, the very beginning of our life in the village. At that time, Poki was in the 4th grade. He ran to our house every day after school. Soon he stopped going to school altogether, and spent his waking hours at our house.

Often, even before we sat down to breakfast, Poki arrived and went directly to the study where he waited for Jim to finish eating. Then, using the feeble English he knew, helped Jim learn his language.

After a few months, they began translating the Book of Genesis. Poki grew excited as he learned about God. One day he said to Jim: "I want this God to be my God!" That day, sitting at the translation table, Poki accepted Jesus.

Too excited to keep his decision to himself, Poki began teaching the older people every Sunday morning, the ones who could not walk easily to Sakarina for church services.

God used Poki's teaching to bring the Managalasi people into His light. Many ceased worshipping ancestor spirits while others pondered the new concepts they were hearing.

One day, while translating the Scriptures, Poki said to Jim: "I want this God to be my God."

Poki planted good seed, readying his people for God's perfect timing.

I remember sitting at the dining room table with Poki one day after Tanya had left the village and returned to the U.S. "Tanya misses the birds singing in the trees," I told him. "In America there aren't any birds singing when she wakes up in the morning."

When Poki didn't respond right away, I glanced at him — he was crying! "Her home is really here in Numba Village," he managed, "but she can't live here anymore." With those words he covered his eyes and sobbed. "I miss her, Rick and Randy so much," he explained between tear-choked spasms. "It's hard to visit you like I used to … it hurts me too much to think about your kids." His deep emotion reinforced to me just how deeply he loved our family.

The next morning we left by helicopter. Mercifully, there were no dramatic goodbyes or wailing, making it easier for me to push aside thoughts that I would not see these friends again until eternity.

A friend in California, whom we called "Uncle John," provided us a home in Huntington Beach close to The Seed Company office, an affiliate of Wycliffe Bible Translators, where we would volunteer.

Jim returned to Numba Village without me for six weeks every January to help Pastor Michael set up the school for the year. Jim helped prepare supplies, like stockpiling enough food for some 130 students to eat two meals daily. He also booked flights for the teachers who flew in from Australia and America.

Unlike our first trip to the isolated village in 1962, technology nowadays allowed Jim to communicate with me over the ocean by phone. Since I wouldn't be accompanying Jim on his trips, he reported daily how the classes were progressing.

"Instead of working in their gardens during the breaks," Jim revealed one day, "many students are going out preaching the Word in other villages. Others who have to stay home and work are sharing what they've learned with the people in their home churches. I already have ten applications for the new school year!"

The school's fame continued to spread, and soon students from several villages outside the Managalasi area were also attending classes.

The first graduating class.

Gene Cunningham and Logan Carnell taught the very first course in 2003 to 48 students. Some sessions were two weeks in duration, others three. Jim scheduled a few weeks' break in-between sessions so students could go home and tend the fields that fed their families.

One October afternoon after Jim and I had been helping in The Seed Company office, we received a phone call from Pastor Roger Thiele who happened to be teaching in the Ese Bible Institute at the time.

"I've got some bad news," he began.

Jim and I braced ourselves.

"Poki died today with Tuberculosis. He's been sick

for about a month and knew he was dying. He gave me a message to give you:

> *"Jim and Jaki, I'm sorry I can't see your faces in Numba one more time, but I'll see you again in heaven. Thank you for coming to our village so I and my people can know the truth and have eternal life. This makes me not afraid to die because I'll go to be with Jesus in heaven. I'll wait for you there. Your son, Poki."*

Now, through tears, Jim and I thought about Poki, our gift from God — always so full of life and contagious laughter. God's Word in his language led him to the Savior he now enjoys in person.

How we wished we could have witnessed Poki's welcome into heaven, to have heard the angels singing. What a day of rejoicing it must have been!

"He was faithful to the One who appointed him ...."
Hebrews 3:2 (NASB)

"All over the world this Gospel is bearing fruit and growing, just as it has been doing among you since the day you heard it and understood God's grace in all its truth." Colossians 1:6 (NIV)

"Iji vu'a maiu'ina kajara joni roa ja'ina'e u'o 'e'une kwaa ararakino va'e hine majaa 'ina renu 'ee rausahe emarenu. 'Ene ni areri vea ka'ene ja Godoni maiji vwihanie ijihuni nimaiji hene kavume rena ja'ina'e renu." Korasia 1:6

Chapter 31

An Addenda

"*We want to keep on learning,*" the students told Jim after the first seminar ended. However, beginning a Bible School would be more than Jim and I could handle alone, so we welcomed Bible scholar Gene Cunningham to help develop the school as well as supply teachers from Australia and America to teach the various courses.

<u>A Word from Some of the Teachers:</u>

Gene Cunningham: "One of the things that impressed me when I first started teaching the Managalasis was a hunger of the students. Other places we go to teach—in Africa or India—the students are reluctant to ask questions. Here in Numba Village the students have all kinds of questions—they want to know *everything!*

"I can see the real desire in their lives to learn the Word and understand it accurately. In-between each course it's their desire to take God's Word out and teach it. To see the hunger of the students and their desire to learn, to grow, and to minister, convinces me that God is doing something special in this place."

Nan Cunningham: "I've made many trips to Numba Village, and my husband and I are so amazed and encouraged by the work God is doing through the Ese Bible Institute. The need I saw that I could fill was to teach the children, the women, and to train Sunday School teachers.

"With help from the members of our church in Australia, we put together a one-year curriculum that teachers can use in their churches throughout the plateau. I began teaching them how to evangelize children, how to teach children, and how to teach them to memorize verses. Then I handed out the curriculums to use. It's been a wonderful experience to return the following year and see the Sunday Schools growing, to see the teachers trained, to see a fire in their hearts to go out to other villages and reach children with the Gospel. I feel this is a way I can support the Bible Institute — by raising up children while they're young so that when they get older they'll be ready and more prepared to enter the Bible Institute.

"One of the more rewarding things for me came right after the first training session. The head of the Sunday School came up to me and said: 'For 15 years I have been in charge of the Sunday School in Numba. And for 15 years I have been praying that God would send some help. Now God has answered my prayer and the help has come.' That was an amazing reward — to see that we were fulfilling a need the village had."

Logan Carnel: "I come from California, the land of plenty. I have a wonderful wife and go to a great church where the Word of God is taught. Taking all that teaching and keeping it to myself didn't seem like what God wanted me to do.

"One day a newsletter came from Gene Cunningham of *Basic Bible Training Ministries*. It asked: 'Where are the Christian adventurers? Where is the same spirit that won the west? Where is that same spirit for Christ?'

"Something about the questions in that letter bothered me, so I kept it in my pocket for six months. One day my wife Desiree, in need of a vacation, wanted to travel. I told her to plan the trip so that we'll see this man Gene Cunningham in Perth, Australia because I want to find out what this call is all about.

"So we went and met up with Gene and his wife Nan. I said, 'We're ready! We want to be Christian Adventurers, too. We want to take everything God has given us and share it with the world. We want to see what Matthew 28:19 is all about — going, therefore, and making disciples of all the nations.'"

"Okay," Gene said. "I think the place to start would be Papua New Guinea. Let's go to Numba!"

"So Desiree and I followed Gene and Nan to Numba Village. Once we arrived I immediately saw the love of Christ in the people of that place. I saw peace, a lack of fear. I saw the teaching that they've had previously come out on their lives. Right away I knew it would be a real honor to be a part of the process.

"I taught one of the ten courses in the Bible Institute and

found the people just so hungry for God. There were many questions asked, they always wanted to know more and more and more. As I taught them, I'd see the lights go on, and the excitement—they would clap and cheer. I wish I saw that same excitement for God back in my own country.

"One night as I was chatting with some of the students, they asked me where my favorite place to visit was. By this time, I had travelled with Gene and Nan to Pakistan, India and Africa. To answer their question, I had to say 'right here in Numba.' I wasn't just saying that to make them happy. Without a doubt, Numba Village is the place where you see God's work coming to fruition. I've never seen it anywhere else in the world."

Desiree Carnell: "Since my husband Logan stays busy teaching in the Ese Bible Institute, I wanted to keep busy teaching God's Word, too, so I began teaching women and children. After our first few trips to Numba, God put it on my heart to go to other hard-to-reach villages which would require several hours of walking.

"One of my favorite places is a village called Jururaha. It's about a six hour walk from Numba, and the people are amazing. They invited me to speak, not only to the children, but to the women as well. In the room where we held our meeting, they proudly demonstrated to me how they knew all the Books of the Bible and many Bible verses.

"After I finished teaching, we ate lunch together. As we ate, they told me how no one from America has ever visited them since Jim went in the early 1970's. They were so thankful and appreciative that I came.

"I also visited another village where no one else had taught, and they received the Word with open hearts, even asking me to leave lessons for them to study on their own. Now, when I go to these far-off villages, I take over 2,500 verses in English translated into Managalasi to share, as well as preparing Bible lessons to teach.

"I see in the people of Papua New Guinea their love for God, and I count it a privilege to serve Him there."

 **Joe Anderson:** "One thing I've learned from the people in Numba Village is living a life of faith. I've studied the Scripture a lot, especially about what it means to have faith during trials. But when I arrived here, I saw these people put their faith into action. They're going through a terrible trial right now since the flood came through their village and the lives of many relatives were lost. But when you talk to them about the Lord, they are excited to hear about how they can serve God during this trial.

"Even in the midst of their trial, I saw some people collecting food to donate to other villages whose loss in their gardens was great. These people from Numba are so generous regardless of their own poverty.

"The other day I asked a lady if I could buy a necklace she had made, and she insisted on giving it to me. They're in such great need, yet in spite of that, they're very generous. And it's been a joy to see that.

"During the Sunday morning church service, I spoke on facing trials from the Books of James and the Gospel of John. They were so excited to hear it, yet in light of their faith right after the flood that claimed lives, I felt inadequate teaching them. What I mean is, I don't have any trials compared to what they've gone through. So it's a real lesson for me to be able to come here and learn from these people when I thought I was coming here to teach them.

"Another thing I've noticed is just how quickly you can develop relationships with them. One man, Ahausa, has become like a brother to me. His father Chululu called me 'his son,' the other day.

"I'll be leaving Numba in a few days, and I feel like I'll be losing friends I've known for a long time."

<u>A Word from Some of the Students:</u>

Thompson: "I come from Kohara Church where I pastor about 90 Christians. Since attending the Bible Institute, I have seen many people in this Province come to know the real Gospel.

"There are three different groups of people here on the plateau — the Anglican church, the Renewals and the Christian Revival Crusade (CRC). Yet, we have unity, and God is doing something great in this province.

"This is especially meaningful to me, because years ago, people all over the world, even in our own nation, looked down on us Managalasi people. They called us 'cannibals' and 'uncivilized.' They even gave us the name 'Managalasi', which means 'empty heads' in the trade language. The whole world looked down on us as primitive people who live far away from main centers. And so my question is, *Why did this Bible School come to the Managalasi people?*

"I have a great challenge from Matthew 20:16 where it says that the last will be first, and the first will be last. If we Managalasi people are considered to be the last people by the world, why should this Gospel reach a third world country first — before other civilized countries and world-established nations?

"Because it's a fulfillment of the Gospel! I'm really encouraged ... and I'm really blessed.

"And this is the challenge I have: To share the Gospel of Jesus Christ with the world until the end time, or until the Rapture takes us Home. Or when death comes to my life, and I'm with the Lord.

"I have a great dream to become a missionary, and it's been the prayer that I've been praying since the year 1999. But I don't know how to start, so that's why I'm here taking this course.

"When going through the seminar on Revelation, our teacher has been telling me that I have to reach my own people at the same time as other nations, at the same time as the world. And so I am challenged to go back to my village and start off with my own people.

"There is an encouraging word that I have received from the apostle Paul: His ministry was from house to house. So when I leave Numba and go home, I will start my new ministry from house to house until I reach some parts of the province, the nations, and even the world.

"If it's God's plan, as Isaiah said, 'Here I am. Send me.'"

Gilbert from Dea Village: "In the year 2001 there was a seminar at Numba Village conducted by Jim Parlier and his wife Jaki. I attended so I could learn how to teach young people better.

"Even though I was a leader, I did not know how to teach properly. That's what brought me to the seminar. During the first session I saw that it was faith alone in Jesus Christ that saved people. I learned many other things, like how God loves us, and how to minister the Gospel to people.

"After the course finished, I knew that God had changed me through His Word. When I went back to my local church and ministered to the youth, I could tell I was a different person.

"When my family heard about the love of God, they believed, and I saw life-changing in them, too. Then, it was very exciting to minister the Word of God to the youth. Some of the young people got so excited, they came to Numba and enrolled to attend the school. They want to hear more about Christ and His love.

"And it's a great joy to be here at the Ese Bible Institute. After I graduated, I returned for every session of the advanced training so I could understand the entire truth of the Bible — to share with my family, my local church, and to reach out to the world.

Chululu from Numba Village: "I am overjoyed that the Ese Bible Institute is established in my village. I see that the school is different, and the things we are taught are wonderful. The teachers who come to teach us don't just teach what they think, but they teach what is in the Word of God.

"I know that mere man didn't establish this school, but it was God. And I can see in the students who attend that their understanding is growing. And because of this, their anger towards other villages, the disagreements and fighting is finishing. Today we have become unified in our beliefs, and we go out teaching God's Word together. The truths we are taught in the school go out through us and help others. We build up *all* the churches inside the plateau and encourage them to be stronger.

"Because of the Bible School, *the churches* are now working together and getting along well. When the school first came, the people living along the plateau believed in different doctrines. The Truth was not taught in their churches. When the students came to attend school, the things they learned helped them to understand the Truth. The students who came to the school had different beliefs at first, but since they've been in the Bible Institute, they hear the Truth being taught every day. That's why they now believe the things they didn't know before — the Truth.

"The students will go from this Bible Institute back to their churches and forget about the denominational teachings being taught in the churches. Instead, they will teach the things they have learned in the school, and they'll go and teach in all the churches so others will hear and know the Truth, too.

"Many students want to start their own churches and teach people how to be saved, that Jesus is coming soon. What I see in this school is that the students are becoming strong in their faith. In the beginning, they didn't know that their beliefs were wrong; they didn't understand that they were teaching concepts that were not true.

"Now I really see that their lives have changed. I hear students saying, 'Oh, we didn't understand before. Now that we came to this school, there has been a new change, a new belief in God's Word. And we will go out and teach everyone this same truth.'"

"It is the same with My Word. I send it out, and it always produces fruit. It will accomplish all I want it to, and it will prosper everywhere I send it." Isaiah 55:11 (NIV)

"Ena'omo Nuni Irijaho ika'ina Nara Ira ka'ene ve'amaro ranave va'amajaho eha pa'a vuata pa'unama rohuna kaivo Nara Ira ka'ene re'urono ranavujaho vuhuna. Ene mamaa marasahi'ina'e rene pituvi'ina'e rehuna." Aisea 55:11

Epilogue

I often thought about that long-ago day in the airport when I had to lay aside my overwhelming desire to stay home with my family rather than board the plane. That was the day Jim and I would be returning to Papua New Guinea for a five-year term. If I had had my way, I would have abandoned the flight and accompanied my sons and daughter back home.

But I knew better: Even though I was torn in two, I knew I had to give God His way and step onto that plane. Now, looking back, I can see that being in that heart-breaking situation was one of God's tools that allowed me to become the person I needed to be in order to fulfill His will for my life.

The remote villages where more than 10,000 Managalasi people lived seemed a million miles from civilization. Tales of cannibalism kept tourists outside the area. In the year 1962, when Jim and I first arrived, law and order had already been established. The people who lived in these villages had never heard the Gospel; there was no word for God in their language. It would be up to us, Jim and me, to teach them who God was.

The Managalasis lived in fear of their ancestor spirits. Failure to please them could mean starvation, sickness, or even death. Believing the spirits attacked at night, as soon as it grew dark, the Managalasis sat huddled together around their fires and did not venture outside until morning's light. Fear held them like prisoners, and their lives were centered around praying to ancestor spirits and appeasing them in every way possible.

Jim built us a house of bamboo walls and flooring in Numba Village. The men helped by cutting off large palm tree branches for a roof. After our house was finished, we spent the day-light hours learning to speak the Managalasi language. We collected hundreds of words on paper and, using these words, devised an alphabet. I then made primers from which the Managalasi people could learn to read.

First, I tried to persuade the men to come to literacy classes.

"Will learning to read help our gardens grow?" one man asked.

"Reading is for you Americans," another concluded. "We have to do work in our gardens every day or we'll be hungry and starve."

When the men could not understand the value of learning to read, I taught women. The ladies were faithful to come every morning and they learned quickly. After about four months, they were able to read any material I handed them. That's what convinced the men: when they saw women looking at paper and saying their Managalasi words, they understood what reading was. This revelation motivated them to come to class and learn.

I used to think that miracles stopped happening after Jesus rose from the dead. Despite my erroneous belief, God used miracles to bring these people *out of darkness*. As they listened to His Word, the Holy Spirit gave them understanding, and they ceased worshipping ancestor spirits. They hungered to learn more about what the Bible taught. Because of their eagerness and strong desire to know God's Word, there is a Bible School in Numba Village today.

The Ese Bible Institute is unique and very much loved by the students. At present, the attendees represent nine languages and five denominations. Many graduates are making an impact through teaching in their churches and villages.

An advanced course has been added to the school curriculum so graduates can return each session and continue to learn.

Some villages have totally changed because, through the graduates and students, they heard the Truth being taught and believed.

"We were believing a lie," some admitted, "but you showed us the Truth from God's Book." These encounters resulted in many men and some women from outside areas enrolling in the Ese Bible Institute. God continues to call some to be pastors, teachers, youth leaders, evangelists, and missionaries. Russell is one example:

One day in EBI class, God spoke to me about giving His Word to lost people.

"I was bored just sitting around in my village doing nothing," Russell told us, "so I enrolled in the Bible Institute. One day in class God spoke to me about giving His Word to lost people. That day I committed my life to Christ to become a missionary and go wherever He led me."

True to his word, after Russell graduated, he travelled over mountainous terrain from village to village teaching the Gospel. He never took provisions with him, but ate and slept out on the narrow trails trusting God to provide.

In 2015, Russell organized a workshop for over 200 young people from various villages. He taught them that by admitting they are sinners and asking Jesus to come into their hearts and cleanse them, they would have eternal life. At the same time they would become a child of God, and, therefore, a part of His family.

"Some young people realized their failures," he reported to us. "Some accepted Christ, and all of them went home viewing their lives from a new perspective."

Then he surprised us with: "I don't think I'll get married because that might interfere with my evangelistic travels.

"God is my #1 priority."

"to open their eyes,
in order to turn them from darkness to light,
and from the power of Satan to God,
that they may receive forgiveness of sins
and an inheritance among those who are sanctified
by faith in Me." Acts 26:18 (NKJV)

" 'Ejakame a veje puni nia jaraahuna. 'Ene pu nututi hijujaho
are'i kaivo ta'arohe hanaji'iniji roajihuna 'ee Setani oni harura
hari hijujaho are'ika'i Godoni rohuna. 'Ejakamareje sisea
vwihanie arevujaho apene 'ee ea ka'ene nimaa rojajihuna Na
iji pijihujipo aachia ka'ene 'ekahunijaho pu 'u'o ijihuni vaji
'ekahuna 'wimana." Akisi 26:18

CPSIA information can be obtained
at www.ICGtesting.com
Printed in the USA
FSOW04n2339031216
28112FS

9 781945 413919